LICA HOLLMAN

50
HIKES in™

ALASKA'S
CHUGACH STATE PARK

50 Hikes in Alaska's Chugach State Park should open a few eyes to the endless possibilities for day hiking, overnight trips, or real backcountry adventure in a park largely accessible from the road system.

—*Coast Magazine*

An excellent addition to the avid hiker's bookshelf.
—*Alaska Women Speak*

50 HIKES in™

ALASKA'S
CHUGACH STATE PARK

**Shane Shepherd &
Owen Wozniak**

THE
MOUNTAINEERS
BOOKS

Published by
The Mountaineers Books
1001 SW Klickitat Way, Suite 201
Seattle, WA 98134

First printing 2001, second printing 2003, third printing 2004,
fourth printing 2006

Published simultaneously in Great Britain by Cordee, 3a DeMontfort
Street, Leicester, England, LE1 7HD

Manufactured in the United States of America

Project Editor: Christine Ummel Hosler
Editor: Marni Keogh
Maps: Jerry Painter
Series cover and book design: Jennifer LaRock Shontz
Book layout: Mayumi Thompson
Photographs by the authors unless otherwise noted

Cover photograph: *Mountains rising from Turnagain Arm* (Photo courtesy
of Chugach State Park)
Frontispiece: *Climbing through brush above Penguin Creek* (Photo by Owen
Wozniak)

Library of Congress Cataloging-in-Publication Data

Shepherd, Shane, 1975-
    50 hikes in Alaska's Chugach State Park / Shane Shepherd and
  Owen Wozniak.— 1st ed.
      p.   cm.
    Includes index.
    ISBN 0-89886-765-7
    1. Hiking—Alaska—Chugach State Park—Guidebooks. 2. Chugach
State Park (Alaska)—Guidebooks. I. Title: Fifty hikes in Alaska's
Chugach State Park. II. Wozniak, Owen, 1975- III. Title.
GV199.42.A42 C48 2001
917.98'35—dc21

                                                     00-012087
                                                         CIP

 Printed on recycled paper

CONTENTS

Key to Map Symbols and Abbreviations

———	Paved road or highway	—··—	Park boundary
═══	Unpaved road	②	Hike number
-------	Trail	▲	Campground
·······	Route	开	Picnic area
∼	River/stream	↑	Cabin or hut
〰	Glacier	▲	Yurt
⬚	Boulder field	Ⓟ	Parking
▲	Mountain or high point	▪	Building or site
◠	Lake or ocean	— — –	Ski lift

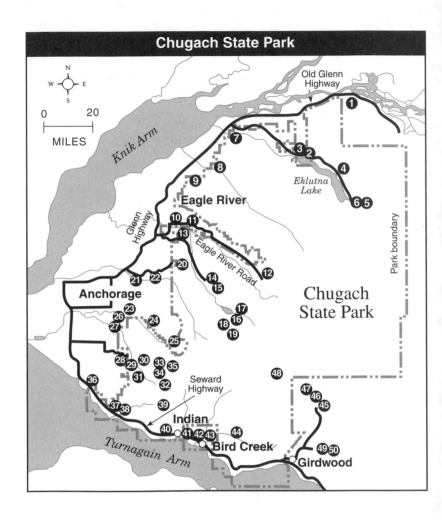

Chugach State Park

W — N — E
S

0 ——— 20
MILES

Knik Arm

Old Glenn
Highway

1

7

3 2

4

8

9

Eklutna
Lake

6 5

Eagle River

Glenn
Highway

10 11

13

Eagle River Road

12

20

14
15

Anchorage

21 22

26 23

24

17

16

18

19

27

25

Chugach
State Park

28

29

30

31

33

34

35

32

48

47

46

45

Park boundary

36

37 38

39

Seward
Highway

40

Indian

41 42 43

44

Turnagain Arm

Bird Creek

49 50

Girdwood

ACKNOWLEDGMENTS

We would like to thank the following people for their help in creating this book: Donna and Morris Shepherd, David and Rachel Wozniak, Bill Sherwonit, Dianne Holmes, Al Meiners and the staff of Chugach State Park, Joann Welch and the Alaska Public Lands Information Center, the staff of the Alaska Room of Loussac Library, the Mountaineering Club of Alaska for access to the Vin Hoeman Library, Joe Walsh for his expert photography tips, Amy Baghramian, Neal Wozniak, Chad and Aaron Shepherd, and Allison Brandt.

Penguin Peak and Turnagain Arm

INTRODUCTION

A WILDERNESS AT OUR DOORSTEP

It's a typical Alaskan summer evening, the ten o'clock sky made vividly pink by the low-hanging sun, and we still have several miles to go. We are following a silty river up its narrowing valley to Eklutna Glacier, hidden from view around a bend. Passing between house-sized boulders, surrounded by soaring, craggy ridges, we climb higher. The temperature drops as we leave the trees and bushes behind. Over the rushing water we hear the glacier groan and crackle. Suddenly, our trail dead-ends at a blank rock face, wet with the river's spray. We can go no further. The glacier has retreated beyond our reach, but we feel its presence in the chill of the wind.

Several days later we climb to a ridge above Eklutna Lake. From this high vantage we can finally see the elusive glacier. It spills into the valley from a tremendous ice field folding into the horizon. Confronted by the vastness of this icy blanket, we imagine the lake below us, the river valley, and even the high ridge on which we stand, buried beneath the weight of that ancient ice. Only recently has Eklutna Glacier ceded this land. Here in the heart of Chugach State Park, with our backs to the city just a few miles away, we peer into a world stuck in geologic time: a land dominated by rivers of ice and vertical rock faces, extending to the edges of our sight.

In Alaska, wilderness is not tucked away in distant national parks. It meets us at the edge of civilization, crowding our communities with mountains and glaciers. Nowhere is this more evident than at Alaska's urban center. In Chugach State Park, a half-million acres of wilderness at the edge of Anchorage, one can lounge at a secluded alpine lake, climb a mountain rising 5000 feet from the sea, and stand in the icy wind of a glacier—all in a day. This accessibility makes the park a wonder, even in a corner of the world cluttered with wonders.

A GUIDE FOR EXPLORING

This book is designed to help you discover the wilderness of Chugach State Park. You'll find everything from marked and maintained trails, to paths cut by the travel of hooves and feet, to hardscrabble routes through brushy valleys and up rocky peaks. As a result, it's not always easy to distinguish between a "trail" and a "possible route." We have therefore attempted to present the "walkable" trails and peaks in the park: the routes where at least some semblance of a trail exists, and the mountains that can be approached and climbed without mountaineering skills.

Winding through cow parsnip and spruce on the Eagle River Trails

Whether you're looking for an easy walk on a nature trail, a demanding cross-country trek to the top of an isolated peak, or something in between, this book will show you where to go. You'll find information on both popular and lesser-known hikes as well as notes about the human and natural history of the area. We tell you how to get to the trailhead, what to expect in the way of terrain and difficulty, and how to link your hike to other routes. This is a guide to help you explore.

Be certain to read the introductory chapters before hitting the trail. They provide crucial tips on safe travel in the wilderness, explanations of the ratings system used to evaluate the trails, information about the park's animal and plant inhabitants, and a brief history of the area. The hike write-ups themselves offer at-a-glance trail data, trailhead directions, and detailed route descriptions. Many hikes are described as out-and-back routes, but we also provide some suggestions for loops and connecting trails. Though rough maps are included, this book is intended to be used alongside topographical maps. *Always carry a map and compass—and make sure you know how to use them.*

PROTECTING OUR WILDERNESS

As the popularity of Alaska's wilderness grows, so does its vulnerability. Every step you take in the backcountry tramples a small part of the tundra; these steps, multiplied by a hundred feet, can easily damage the fragile landscape if care is not taken to stay on trails and off delicate plants. Likewise, nothing spoils a hike more quickly than discovering someone's discarded litter. By entering Chugach State Park, you accept the responsibility to leave the wilderness as unspoiled as you found it. Read the "Leave No Trace" section of this book for information on wilderness ethics. By working together to keep Chugach State Park clean and pristine, we can all enjoy the park's wilderness in the decades to come.

Your greatest resources for enjoying the park are respect for the backcountry, sound judgment, a willingness to explore, and a knowledge of your limitations. Those attributes and this book should get you as far into the wilderness as you want to go—all within an hour's drive from Anchorage. Enjoy!

A NOTE ABOUT SAFETY

Safety is an important concern in all outdoor activities. No guidebook can alert you to every hazard or anticipate the limitations of every reader. Therefore, the descriptions of roads, trails, routes, and natural features in this book are not representations that a particular place or excursion will be safe for your party. When you follow any of the routes described in this book, you assume responsibility for your own safety. Under normal conditions, such excursions require the usual attention to traffic, road and trail conditions, weather, terrain, the capabilities of your party, and other factors. Keeping informed on current conditions and exercising common sense are the keys to a safe, enjoyable outing.

The Mountaineers Books

THE LAND

Chugach State Park contains an amazing diversity of geology, history, and natural life in its 495,000 acres. In this section we offer some insights into the land you will be walking through.

THE FORMATION OF THE LAND

Alaska was not always such a huge place. In fact, when the Chugach Mountains were first formed, they weren't part of Alaska at all! The mountains behind Anchorage were thrust out of the Pacific around 130 million years ago as part of a volcanic island system. Born from the ocean floor, far away from Alaska, they began a long journey across the Pacific tectonic plate toward their future home.

Geologists believe that much of Alaska was assembled from various *terranes*, such as the landmass composing the Chugach Mountains. These large, distinct chunks of land accreted over millions of years against the North American continent, adding their land mass to the mainland. The Chugach terrane reached southern Alaska around 65 million years ago. After docking in Alaska, these mountains continued to grow as the Pacific plate buckled under and lifted the North American plate—a process that continues today.

After these land masses reached their northern location, they were beset by glaciers. At least four major glaciations swept through Southcentral Alaska during the Pleistocene epoch, between 10,000 and 1.6 million years ago. During the Wisconsin stage (the most recent glaciation), glaciers advanced beyond the edges of present-day Anchorage. At the height of the Wisconsin, the entire Chugach State Park (except the tops of the highest peaks) was buried in ice. A global warming led to the retreat of these glaciers around 10,000 years ago. Nowadays, 10 percent of the park remains beneath glaciers, though even these survivors recede a little further every year.

Other forces have contributed to the shaping of the mountains. Water erosion is primary among these, as rivers wear away the mountainsides and carry them in small grains back to the ocean floor from which they came. Earthquakes are another contributing factor: the 1964 Good Friday earthquake, which measured 8.4 on the Richter scale, caused the Chugach Mountains to subside by more than 2 feet. Also still sculpting the mountains today are mechanical weathering (when expanding, freezing water breaks apart rock) and solifluction (the buildup and runoff, in layers, of soil and rocks).

Looking down the Historic Iditarod Trail
above the Crow Creek mine ruins

Terrain Features

Evidence of the park's dynamism is everywhere, perhaps most spectacularly in its many glaciers. These glaciers are not as large as they once were: they advanced during a mini-glaciation until about 1910, but since then a warming climate has caused them to retreat rapidly, some by as much as 75 to 100 feet a year.

Glaciers are sometimes called "rivers of ice." Like rivers, they are pulled downhill by gravity, though at a much slower rate. Also like rivers, they shape the valley through which they flow. As glaciers move, they crush the valley floor and walls beneath their weight, grinding and abrading the rock. Chugach State Park has been well-marked by glaciers, and you'll see signs of their passage even in valleys from which they have long vanished. Most valleys in the park have a U-shape, with flat bottoms and steep walls, distinct from the V-shaped valleys commonly formed by the eroding action of streams.

Glaciers leave other clues to their passing. Have you ever stumbled across a gigantic boulder lying in the middle of a valley floor? You may wonder how these huge rocks arrived at such curious resting spots. These are glacial erratics, gouged bulldozer-like out of the bedrock by an advancing glacier, or perhaps deposited on top of the glacier from a nearby high ridge. The glacier carries these rocks as it advances down the valley; when the glacier melts, the rocks are left behind, strewn haphazardly across the valley floor.

In many valleys you'll also see large piles of rock strangely organized in

Raven Glacier seen from Crow Pass

Greywacke, shown here near Bird Ridge, is a sedimentary rock found throughout Chugach State Park.

a line. These rocks are glacial moraine. Similar to erratics, they are dug up and pushed forward by advancing glaciers. Terminal moraines, generally lying across a valley horizontally, mark the line of a glacier's farthest advance; lateral moraines, which run parallel to the line of the valley, mark the sides of the glacier, while a medial moraine (a rocky spine cleaving a glacier in two) marks a spot where two glaciers converged.

Other glacial leavings include tarns, small alpine lakes that are created when water fills depressions left by retreating glaciers. There are hundreds of these tarns in the park. Many of the park's serrated mountain ridges, called aretes, were also formed by glaciation.

The predominant type of rock you'll see in the Chugach is called "greywacke," a dirty sandstone composed of quartz, feldspar, and various volcanic rocks. Because these rocks are really just hardened oceanic sediment, they're very crumbly, a quality you can't fail to notice when hiking through the mountains. Pick up a loose rock and look at its layered structure. If the rock is thin enough, you'll be able to snap it in two with your bare hands. Keep this in mind when deciding where to climb—these rocks are not much more solid than a handful of silt gathered from the ocean floor.

HUMAN HISTORY

Somewhere between 15,000 and 40,000 years ago, when much of the ocean's water was locked up in ice sheets spreading across North America, humans began a migration from Siberia to Alaska. Ever in pursuit of their next meal, these hunter-gatherers wandered along with their prey, such as the woolly mammoth, across the Bering Land Bridge (not a bridge as we think of it—this swath of land was more than 1000 miles wide!) and found an ice-free paradise in the Alaskan Interior. Rainfall here was too limited for glaciers to form, and the steppe tundra provided plentiful game and shelter. The wetter lands further south were buried in ice, thus preventing the migrants from visiting present-day Cook Inlet for many more millennia. Similarly, glaciers blocked access to the greater North American continent. Locked in a prison of ice, these early nomads, along with the animals they had followed, remained in Alaska's Interior for generations.

Early Eskimos at Beluga Point

Eventually the ice sheets began to retreat, opening a southern migration route. Early Eskimos (who may have actually been Paleo-Indians) arrived in what is now Chugach State Park around 10,000 years ago. Beluga Point, a rocky outcropping along Turnagain Arm, was most likely one of their early encampments. Hunters pursued beluga whales and salmon in the nearby waters, and sheep, goat, and caribou in the mountains. Rocks along the beach provided shelter from the wind, offering a place for Eskimo hunters to build fires to cook their meat and to keep themselves warm. This area was likely used until rather recently: remains of hearths from as little as 600 years ago have been uncovered.

Despite their continual presence, the Eskimo peoples built only seasonal settlements in the area. When these nomads began to establish villages, they eschewed Cook Inlet in favor of more hospitable sites in Prince William Sound and Kachemak Bay. They continued to visit Cook Inlet and Turnagain Arm during the summers to hunt, but fled south with the approach of winter.

Beluga Point on Turnagain Arm, where centuries-old native artifacts have been discovered

The Dena'inas

Not until 1000 years ago did the Dena'ina (de-NINE-ah) Athabascans migrate from Alaska's Interior to Cook Inlet. The Eskimo peoples continued to make summer trips to Cook Inlet to hunt and fish, but by the time James Cook arrived on the scene in 1778 the Dena'inas had firmly supplanted these earlier inhabitants.

The Dena'inas constructed many villages along Cook Inlet and Turnagain Arm, adapting well to the land. The only Alaskan Athabascans to live along saltwater, they had an easier life than their brethren in the Interior. Winters were less harsh, and the sea provided a bountiful source of food. They borrowed technology from the Eskimos, such as the *baidorka* (a type of kayak) and harpoons to hunt belugas, and adapted freshwater fishing methods to suit the extreme tides of Cook Inlet.

The Dena'inas lived off the land and respected its creatures. According to their traditions, when the world began, there was not a great difference between people and animals. The animals lived together with the humans and shared a common language. Many of the animals had distinct personalities. The raven, for instance, had a godlike power and a penchant for pranks. At some point the plants and animals all went through strange transformations, eventually taking on their present shapes. However, they retained their human-like spirits. This causes the Dena'ina to feel a special kinship with living things, as they remember that in the ancient order all the animals were essentially human. The Dena'inas feel that everything in nature possesses its own spirituality. They must show respect toward nature or risk punishment—perhaps bad luck while hunting, illness, or even death.

The Dena'ina way of life is mostly a thing of past; like so many other native cultures in the New World, it did not survive the arrival of Europeans. They held on for a time; when the Russians came to Alaska in the eighteenth century, primarily in pursuit of sea otter pelts, they bypassed Cook Inlet in favor of Kodiak Island and Sitka. Even after President Andrew Johnson's Secretary of State, William Seward, convinced a skeptical Congress to purchase Alaska from the Russians in 1867, Cook Inlet remained unoccupied by non-Natives. But a new discovery would soon energize every part of Alaska and doom the Dena'inas' traditional way of life: gold.

Gold Rushes and Railroads

When the famous British navigator, James Cook, sailed into Cook Inlet in 1778, he was searching for the fabled "Northwest Passage" from Europe to Asia. He diligently charted the coastline and even explored a narrow nearby fjord. When he reached a dead end of mountains and glaciers, he ordered his crew to "turn 'round again," and named the fjord "River Turnagain."

Having offered nothing to either the Russians or the British, Turnagain Arm finally yielded treasure in 1888, when prospectors discovered gold at Sixmile Creek. The next ten years brought gold hunters in droves. Fortunate miners hit small jackpots at several streams in the area, and established moderately productive lode mines at both Indian Creek and Crow Creek. However, the yield from these operations was paltry compared to later strikes in the Klondike and at Nome. By the turn of the century, most of the miners had packed up and headed northward in search of greater riches.

Though short-lived, the Cook Inlet gold rush opened an era of white settlement in the region. The heavy influx of prospectors heading to points north created a need for a reliable overland route. Early travelers would sail into port at Seward and make their way to the Nome gold fields, more than 1000 miles away, along the Historic Iditarod Trail (which cut through the heart of modern-day Chugach State Park). A long and punishing journey, it was especially dangerous at Crow Pass, where avalanches threatened travelers throughout the winter. The establishment of a safer route over Indian Creek Pass added still more distance to an already grueling trip. There was only one adequate solution: Alaska needed a railroad.

The Alaska Central Railroad Company first began surveying the route between Seward and Turnagain Arm in 1903. Harsh weather and uneven terrain made construction highly difficult, and the company completed only 51 miles before going bankrupt. Its successor, the Alaska Northern Railroad, fared even worse. They extended the track only another 20 miles further, to a point just south of Girdwood.

After hearing entreaties from ruined investors, the federal government came to the rescue. In 1915, President Woodrow Wilson issued an executive order to buy the fledging railroad. The government sought to establish a continuous 471 miles of track from Seward to Fairbanks in the hopes of opening the Alaskan Interior to full-scale development. Work along Turnagain Arm was both slow and expensive—each mile of track cost around $200,000 to complete! Many small tent cities sprung up along the route; one of them, located on the mouth of Ship Creek, would later mushroom into Anchorage. Several buildings from the early railroad days remain along the railroad. Among them is Potter Section House, which now serves as headquarters for Chugach State Park.

The railroad was completed in 1922; in 1923, President Warren Harding commemorated the project by driving in a golden spike near Nenana. The Alaska Railroad, the only federally owned railroad in the history of the United States, was sold to the state of Alaska in 1985 and today remains an important link to the Interior.

The Creation of a Park

When Alaska became the forty-ninth state in 1959, the federal government granted the new state more than 100 million acres of land. This bounty included a large tract of wilderness behind Anchorage, by then the state's largest city. Anchorage residents had become accustomed to using this land as an open recreation area, and many feared that the state would sell it to private interests. Indeed, when in 1969 the state announced a timber sale in Indian Creek Valley, many suspected their backyard wilderness was about to be dismantled.

A grassroots organization quickly formed to fight the timber sale. An ad hoc committee, chaired by nineteen-year-old Sharon Cissna, assembled an ambitious plan to preserve the wilderness behind Anchorage by creating a state park. Backed by a large and diverse alliance of local residents, the movement rapidly gained steam. First came an injunction to halt the logging, then the submission of a bill to the Alaska Legislature proposing a state park. The committee asked for the inclusion of as much land as they could possibly think of—a huge area including all the state lands east of Anchorage, north of Girdwood, and south of Knik Arm. Nearly half of Alaska's legislature signed on as co-sponsors of the bill, and when it was signed into law in 1970, the ad hoc committee (to their own surprise) got nearly every square inch of land they had proposed.

Modern Uses

First the home of the Dena'ina, then a place for prospectors to pursue their dreams, the mountains above Anchorage and Turnagain Arm now form the most popular recreational area in Alaska—quite a distinction in a state whose inhabitants pursue outdoor sports at twice the national average. Even before the park's creation, hikers roamed its valleys, mountaineers explored its immense glaciers and remote peaks, and hunters and anglers took their rifles and rods in search of Dall sheep, moose, bears, and salmon. When Bill Hauser edited the state's first hiking guide, *30 Hikes in Alaska*, he included many popular hikes in the Anchorage area. Vin Hoeman, perhaps the region's most prolific explorer, was the first to climb many of the area's peaks. The names he gave these mountains—such as Williwaw, Penguin, and Temptation—reflect his belief that "men should be named after mountains, and not vice-versa." Some of the more remote summits in the park still hold the original registers he placed there more than 30 years ago.

Chugach State Park has steadily increased in popularity since the days of Hoeman and Hauser. Flattop, the most-climbed mountain in Alaska, sees thousands of hikers every year. A restored section of the Historic Iditarod Trail between Girdwood and Eagle River has become a very popular backpacking route. Even the more remote regions of the park are seeing increasing use.

As a result of this popularity, it is increasingly important that Alaskans and visitors to the park treat the land with the utmost respect and care. Three decades ago, the Chugach State Park ad hoc committee worked to ensure Anchorage's backyard wilderness would remain wild and untouched, so that future generations could continue to enjoy its beauty and solitude. Now the task falls to us.

THE PARK'S INHABITANTS: PLANTS AND ANIMALS

For a land lying mostly above the trees, Chugach State Park contains a surprising diversity of plant and animal life. It is home to everything from dense thickets of cow parsnip and alder in boggy valleys, to delicate orange, green, and black lichens atop high peaks, to rockweed and moss in Turnagain Arm's intertidal zone. The park's animals range from grizzly bears to Great Horned owls, from porpoises to pikas. No brief summary can do the park's variety justice; what follows is not a complete list but a selected guide to some of the most prominent flora and fauna you're likely to encounter in the park's various habitats. For a more thorough treatment, see Jenny Zimmerman's *A Naturalist's Guide to Chugach State Park*.

The many different habitats of Chugach State Park, and the plants and animals they support, are influenced by factors such as exposure to sun and wind, precipitation, temperature, and soil composition—all of which vary greatly across the park's half million acres. The following paragraphs describe major habitats, moving upward from the coast to the mountains.

Marine Habitats

The park's marine habitats include coastal wetlands, the intertidal zone, and the waters of Turnagain Arm. It is very dangerous to explore the mud flats or take a swim in Turnagain Arm, but you can frequently spot beluga whales from the Seward Highway. They're also known as "white whales," though these gregarious mammals bear little resemblance to Captain Ahab's sea beast. Belugas are between 11 and 15 feet long and weigh several thousand pounds; the head resembles a bulging melon. The smaller of Alaska's two beluga populations lives in Cook Inlet (the other spends most of its time in the Bering Sea) and makes regular appearances en masse in Turnagain Arm. Also present but more rare are the odd orca, harbor seal, sea lion, and harbor porpoise.

Muskeg

The park's marshy lowlands, known as muskeg, form another distinct habitat. Common in old river bottoms and other poorly drained areas, muskeg hosts a variety of berry bushes, mosses, grasses, willows, and lichens. Alder and scraggly black spruce are abundant. So are mosquitoes, so have bug juice ready if you plan to venture into the muskeg. Other animals include lemmings, muskrats, minks, shrews, voles, blackbirds, sparrows, great blue herons, and the park's only amphibian, the wood frog.

Riparian Habitats

Riparian habitats (those along the edges of lakes and streams) have many of the same plants and animals as muskeg. Look for beavers, river otters, plovers, waterthrushes, Canada geese, mallard and harlequin ducks, and the occasional bald eagle. Keep your eyes peeled for moose as well. Some of the larger rivers and lakes have Dolly Varden and rainbow

Muskeg and open water at Potter Marsh

trout, while the streams emptying into Turnagain Arm teem with salmon and the less exalted hooligan fish.

Coniferous Forests

Coniferous forests fill much of the southern park's lowlands. Populated mainly by western hemlock and Sitka spruce, the forests lining the eastern half of Turnagain Arm represent the northernmost extension of Southeastern Alaska's great temperate rain forest. Trees tower more than a hundred feet high, blocking out the sunlight. The forest floor, mired in perpetual dampness, supports a profusion of shade-tolerant undergrowth such as stairstep moss, oak and deer ferns (the latter rising several feet high), and a wide variety of mushrooms.

Other inhabitants include the infamous devil's club, a deciduous shrub characterized by wide, spiky leaves and a spiny stem, often growing in thick clumps along the trail, and cow parsnip, marked by large, three-sectioned, palm-like leaves and small white flowers growing in clusters at the end of thick, woody stems. Both plants, common throughout the park, sometimes grow to head-height or above, and both can cause itching, scrapes, and rashes. They tend to limit the allure of bushwhacking through the deep forest. The more benign plant life includes fireweed (named not for the bright red color taken on by its leaves in autumn, but instead because its horizontal root network makes it somewhat fire-resistant), dwarf dogwood (look for four white petals on the flower), and Jacob's ladder (a tall flowering plant with five violet petals).

Coniferous forests support a variety of animals as well, including moose, bears, porcupine, and even lynx, the park's only cat. Lynx feed primarily on snowshoe hares and squirrels, the latter of which you're unlikely to miss on any visit to the woods. Most of the bears here are black bears, though you might also see grizzlies. Birds include juncos, sparrows, flycatchers, goshawks, saw-whet owls, grosbeaks, Steller's jays, and woodpeckers. Also hard to miss is the spruce grouse, a plump, chicken-like bird that remains oblivious to approaching hikers until it's practically been stepped on.

Mixed Forests

You'll find mixed forests in drier areas of the park. Trees tend to be shorter, thanks in part to reduced precipitation. The principal trees are white and black spruce (both smaller than the Sitka spruce), paper birch, quaking aspen (its small and roundish green leaves often trembling in the breeze), poplar, and willow. At higher elevations the birch generally disappear, replaced by thickets of alder and open meadows.

The forest understory is similarly dense and diverse, supporting flowers such as Labrador tea, spirea, cinquefoil, and lowbush cranberry. Devil's club, cow parsnip, willow, mountain ash, and lupine are also common.

Mixed forests support many of the same animals as coniferous forests, including moose, bears, porcupines, and martens. Look also for red foxes, weasels, and the elusive northern flying squirrel, gliding from tree to tree (though you'll be lucky to witness such a flight, as it is a nocturnal animal). Birds include a variety of thrushes, warblers, sparrows, and chickadees. Magpies and robins are also frequently observed.

Subalpine Areas

Subalpine areas, characterized by thickets of alder, willow, mountain ash, and juniper, form another common—and often impenetrable—habitat of Chugach State Park. As the name implies, subalpine areas are generally found around tree line, though similar habitats exist along some riverbanks and coastal areas of the park. Many of the open forest bird species listed above flourish in the thickets, protected from predators by the dense warren of branches. Among mammals, moose are common. Weighing in around 1000 pounds and standing more than 6 feet at the shoulder, they are the largest members of the deer family. Constantly in search of tender willow, birch, and alder branches, the park's several hundred moose tend to roam mountain forests and valleys during summer and migrate down toward Anchorage during winter.

Alpine Tundra

Last but certainly not least is the park's most abundant habitat: alpine tundra. A wide-open land above the trees, tundra is composed of low shrubs and flowers such as bell and mountain heather, bromegrass, mountain avens, blueberry, crowberry, lowbush cranberry, dwarf fireweed, woolly lousewort, western buttercup, alpine meadow bistort, and Alaska's state flower, the delicate blue forget-me-not. Lower, boggier tundra is rich in mosses and shrubs; small wildflowers and the occasional sideways-growing conifer, called krumholz, populate higher, windswept tundra. Scree slopes, cliffs, and even mountaintops host a variety of orange, white, green, and black lichens.

Living among this rugged flora are some of the park's most graceful and elusive animals. Most of the park's approximately forty grizzly bears live on and around the tundra, feeding on ripe berries, mice, voles, and just about anything else they can find. It takes a lot of land to feed a grizzly—a single animal's home range can cover hundreds of square miles. A more abundant but equally beautiful animal, the Dall sheep lives almost entirely above tree line on south-facing slopes. Around Turnagain Arm, in Ram Valley, at East Twin Pass, in Ewe Valley, and elsewhere, Dall sheep can be seen in great numbers, moving agilely across the slopes. Less common are mountain goats, pointy-horned and larger than Dall sheep, who live near rock outcroppings and generally keep to the coastal alpine areas.

Rocky areas are also home to the pika, a small rodent-like creature measuring around 8 inches. They make a distinctive chirping sound, especially when a hiker has disturbed their dens among the boulders of a talus slope. Hoary marmots, known for their whistle, also live among the rocks. You might spot one standing upright, guarding its den, or lounging on a warm rock in summer.

Wolverines and coyotes also live on the tundra, though you're unlikely to see them. The same is true for the wolf, possibly the most magnificent of all the creatures in the park. Wolves are generally gray (though sometimes white or black) and large, sometimes rising 3 feet at the shoulder. They live in packs roaming from the forests to the tundra year-round.

Such a variety of habitats in close proximity makes for a wealth of hiking experiences. A single hike can lead from ocean to rain forest to alpine desolation and back. The land is sometimes wet, lush, and overgrown, sometimes rocky, barren and windswept. Nearly always rugged and rarely trafficked, its diversity is part of what makes Chugach State Park such a challenging and continually rewarding place to explore.

Dall sheep

PARK FACILITIES AND RULES

Before heading into Chugach State Park, take a moment to familiarize yourself with its facilities and rules. You'll find picnic areas, campgrounds (both commercial and state-run), and a number of resources for further information.

Park Headquarters: Potter Section House, Mile 115, Seward Highway. Tel: (907) 345-5014

This is the place to ask questions regarding trail conditions, campgrounds, fees, and permits. The headquarters is located in a building preserved from one of the many section camps erected during railroad construction in the 1920s; check out the nine-foot snow blower on the antique train engine parked nearby. Park officials encourage backcountry hikers to register a trip plan here before departing.

The Eagle River Nature Center: Mile 12, Eagle River Road. Tel: (907) 694-2108

Located in the upper Eagle River Valley, the Eagle River Nature Center is a mecca for outdoor enthusiasts of all stripes. In addition to exhibits about the plant and animal life in the park, the center offers a program of talks and group activities, such as mushroom hunts, geology walks, astronomy programs, and guided hikes. They also host regular children's programs for the junior naturalist in your family. A network of trails, including the Historic Iditarod Trail, departs from the nature center; see Hike 12 for more information. The nature center rents and maintains a public-use cabin and two yurts (teepee-like domed tents constructed over wooden platforms and equipped with stoves). You can reserve these year-round by mail, over the phone, in person, or over the Internet at *www.ernc.org*. This website also has a schedule of upcoming programs.

The nature center is run by Friends of the Eagle River Nature Center, a community-supported, non-profit group dedicated to promoting the natural history and recreational use of Chugach State Park. A portion of the proceeds from the sale of this book are being donated to Friends of the Eagle River Nature Center; if you've enjoyed one of their programs or use of the Eagle River trails, consider making a donation as well.

FEES

Due to state funding cuts, user fees are now crucial to the park's survival. If there is a fee, pay it! The fee for day parking is $5, and annual

A front-door view that can't be beat: camping in the backcountry. (Photo courtesy of Chugach State Park)

Visitors gather for an interpretive program at the Eagle River Nature Center. (Photo courtesy of Chugach State Park)

passes (a good deal if you'll be visiting a fee area more than a few times a year) are available for $25 at the park headquarters. Camping fees are assessed at all three drive-in campgrounds, and you may also have to pay a fee for sanitary dumping, firewood, and reserved use of cabins or group camping areas.

CAMPGROUNDS

The park maintains public drive-in campgrounds at Eagle River, Bird Creek, and Eklutna Lake. They are generally open from May 1 through September 15. The campsites have picnic tables, fire pits, water, and toilets, and are limited to two vehicles, two tents, and twelve people. Camping fees range from $10 to $15 per night, and annual passes are also available for resident Alaskans. Park hosts oversee the campgrounds and are happy to offer assistance and answer questions.

Bird Creek (mile 100, Seward Highway): This campground is ideal for accessing trailheads along Turnagain Arm from Potter to Girdwood. It has twenty-two units plus an overflow area; stay is limited to 7 days. You'll find groceries in Bird, but for camping supplies (stove fuel, raingear, etc.), get outfitted in Anchorage. It's a short walk to Bird Creek, where fishermen attempt to get away from it all with several hundred of their fellow anglers, crowding shoulder to shoulder on the riverbank. Tangled lines, lures cast willy-nilly, slippery tackle spilling everywhere, and a little too much beer make for a uniquely Alaskan sport known to many as "combat fishing."

Eagle River (mile 12, Glenn Highway): Eagle River Campground is a busy place, with river access for fishing and rafting, and proximity to trailheads in Eagle River Valley. Driving north on the Glenn Highway from Anchorage, take the Hiland Road exit and turn left; follow the signs along the frontage road to the campground. It boasts flush toilets and fifty camping units plus an overflow area; stay is limited to 4 days. Just about all of your outfitting needs can be met in Eagle River.

Eklutna Lake (mile 26, Glenn Highway): On the western shore of Eklutna Lake, this campground lies at the start of Eklutna's hiking trails. Eklutna is also a popular destination for boaters, so expect crowds on summer weekends. Take the Eklutna exit at mile 26 on the Glenn Highway and follow the signs for the lake road, which runs 10 miles to the lake. The main campground has fifty regular units, a large-group campsite, and handicapped-accessible and overflow units. Along the Lakeside Trail (open to motorized all-terrain vehicles Sunday through Wednesday, and to cyclists and hikers every day) you'll find two additional, little-used campgrounds, each with six units, and a public-use cabin and public-use hut available by reservation (see Hike 2 for more information). For most sup-

A picnic site at the Eagle River Campground

plies, you'll likely need to stop in Eagle River, although there is a small general store on the approach road.

Backcountry Camping

Chugach State Park boasts an endless supply of beautiful backcountry campsites. Please do your best to minimize your campsite's environmental impact. Fires are generally prohibited in the park (see below) and you should always bear-bag your food before retiring for the night (see the "Bears" section of this introduction for a brief how-to on bear-bagging). Established campsites along the Historic Iditarod Trail (Hike 45) and the Eklutna Lakeside Trail (Hike 2) are available on a first-come basis.

Fires

Fires are permitted *only* in campground fire pits and along the gravel bars of Eklutna Lake, Peters Creek, Bird Creek, and Eagle River below the high-water mark. You may use only "dead and down" wood, and you should keep all fires small. At the drive-in campgrounds, firewood is usually available for a fee at the host campsite. In all non-emergency situations, please strongly consider using a camp stove instead of building a fire.

Picnic Areas

The park maintains picnic sites at its Eagle River and Eklutna Campgrounds, at McHugh Creek State Wayside (see Hike 37), and at Upper Huffman Trailhead (see Hike 27).

Cabins

The park maintains two cabins for public use at Eklutna Lake. The first is on Yuditna Creek near mile 3 of the Eklutna Lakeside Trail. It is 12 feet by 16 feet and sleeps six, maximum eight. The second, the Serenity Falls hut, lies at mile 12 on the Lakeside Trail. It is divided into three sections, each with space for four to six people. Reserve either cabin in person or by mail at the Department of Natural Resources Public Information Center, located at 550 West Seventh Avenue, Twelfth Floor, Anchorage, AK 99501. Reservations are first-come, first-served, can be made for up to three consecutive nights or one weekend per month, and are taken up to six months in advance. You can check on availability by calling the Public Information Center at (907) 269-8400 (then press 0) or on the Internet at *www.state.ak.us* (follow the links under "Hot Topics" to the Public-Use Cabins page).

The U.S. Forest Service maintains a cabin at Crow Pass, which offers superb access to many peaks and trails in and around Chugach State Park. To reserve it, call (800) 280-2267. It is often booked well in advance.

The Eagle River Nature Center maintains a cabin and two yurts, complete with stoves and available for year-round rental. Call (907) 694-2108 for more information or reserve them through their website at *www.ernc.org*.

MOTOR VEHICLES

No vehicles may be operated off established roads and parking areas except where designated. The use of snow and all-terrain vehicles (four-wheelers, etc.) is strictly regulated: operators must be 14 years or older unless directly supervised by someone age 21 or older. Proof of age may be requested. Most areas of the park are off-limits to these vehicles.

MOUNTAIN BIKING

Although the park is largely closed to bikes, several trails allow mountain biking. These are mainly wide dirt roads and do not provide the most challenging biking, but they will get you into the backcountry on two wheels. Biking is allowed on the Eklutna Lakeside Trail, Peters Creek Road, the logging roads around Bird Creek (beware of overgrown trails!), the Near Point Trail (from Prospect Heights Trailhead to the end of the homestead roadbed, 2½ miles up the trail), the Powerline Trail, the Gasline Trail, and the River Woods Trail.

EMERGENCIES

In the case of emergencies, call 911, the Anchorage Police at (907) 786-8500, or the Alaska State Troopers at (907) 428-7200.

BEFORE YOU GO

Chugach State Park draws hikers for its accessible wilderness. Although beautiful, it can also turn dangerous, sometimes just beyond the trailhead. Storms sometimes rise quickly, even at the height of summer; a wrong turn on a poorly marked trail may lead to hours of frustrating bushwhacking; an ankle sprain may necessitate an unexpected overnight bivouac. Treat this wilderness with respect and come prepared. Every time you set foot in the park, make sure you have proper food, clothing, and navigational aids, and the ability to use them.

WHAT TO BRING

The classic outdoor textbook *Mountaineering: The Freedom of the Hills* lists "Ten Essentials" everyone should carry *on every hike*. They are:
- Extra clothing, including several non-cotton layers, a rain shell, and a warm hat.
- Extra food, at least a day's worth for overnight hikes.
- Sunglasses. These are especially important at higher altitudes and on snow, where the sun's glare can quickly cause snow blindness. This is true even on cloudy days.
- A basic first-aid kit. Don't just buy one and toss it in your pack—make sure you know what it contains and how to use it. You won't need a snakebite kit in Alaska.
- A pocketknife.
- Matches in a waterproof container.
- A fire starter, such as dry tinder or a candle.
- Flashlight or headlamp, with an extra bulb and batteries. This is less important during Alaska's summer days of midnight sunshine, but it may come in handy for an unplanned bivouac.
- A detailed topographical map. Make sure it includes the full area of your hike.
- A compass.

Additionally, you should carry plenty of water and/or a water purifier. Check to see if water is available along the trail before you depart; the descriptions for each hike generally note if you'll have a difficult time finding drinking water.

Choose you footwear carefully, lest blisters turn an otherwise pleasant hike into a painful plod. Most hikers wear heavy boots with lug soles and a double layer of socks (a thin pair of synthetic liner socks underneath heavier

A moose browses the undergrowth near McHugh Creek State Wayside.

wool or synthetic socks). Lightweight hiking shoes are fine for easygoing trails but put your ankles at risk on rocky terrain. Muddy trails lined with wet brush make waterproof boots highly desirable. All of your clothing should be non-cotton, generally a polyester blend or wool. Bring a waterproof outer shell made of coated nylon or, ideally, a breathable fabric like Gore-Tex.

A knapsack with the Ten Essentials, a hearty lunch, and 2 liters of water should suffice for most day hikes. On overnight outings, bring a full pack with appropriate camping gear (see Appendix B for a checklist).

Finally, keep in mind the advice of Chugach State Park Superintendent Al Meiners: "The best piece of gear you can take with you is what you carry between your ears." We've all forgotten essential equipment before, but your common sense is the one thing you can't afford to leave sitting on the kitchen table.

WEATHER

Summer weather in Chugach State Park can change quickly; come prepared for a possible storm, even on the sunniest days. Midsummer temperatures usually range from the mid 40s to the high 70s. Above tree line expect colder temperatures and strong winds. Nighttime temperatures may drop below freezing on the tundra.

These discouraging scenarios notwithstanding, the park actually provides many days of near-ideal hiking weather during the summer. Torrential rain is rare, as are thunder and lightning storms. Cloudy days are often cool and slightly moist, making for comfortable hiking conditions. Even on rainy days the evenings often clear up to reveal fiery sunsets. And when clear skies prevail, providing views from the Kenai Mountains to Denali, you won't find a more inviting place than the Chugach high tundra.

WATER PURIFICATION

It looks crisp and pure, but that mountain water advertised on TV is far from clean—even in Alaska. A microorganism called *Giardia lamblia*, found in mountain goat and beaver excrement, commonly makes its way into streams near the alpine source. It can cause giardiasis ("beaver fever") when it camps out in your small intestine, resulting in constant diarrhea, gas, bloating, and abdominal cramps. All water you drink in the park should be considered suspect and properly treated before consumption.

There are three ways to purify water in the backcountry: boiling, filtration, and chemical treatment. Boiling is the most effective method. Boil water for at least 1 minute, longer if it comes from a lake or beaver pond. This is not always convenient, but it's the only sure-fire way to measure up to Anchorage's tap water.

You can also purify water with a mechanical filter, available at most outdoor stores. Filters with a pore size of 0.4 micrometers or less are needed to strain out giardia. While quick to use, filters are usually expensive and bulky. Furthermore, some filters exhibit a frustrating habit of clogging or breaking in the backcountry.

Many hikers opt for chemical treatment, usually with iodine in a solution or tablet form. Iodine tablets are lightweight and easy to pack, and, in most cases, giardia protozoa and giardia cysts are destroyed by iodine. However, iodine is not 100 percent effective against giardia and there have been recent reports of iodine-resistant giardia cysts. To protect yourself against giardia, double the prescribed dose or double the recommended 20-minute waiting time. If the water comes from a particularly cold source, such as a glacial stream, you should treat it longer. See your product's specific instructions. Iodine leaves a less than refreshing aftertaste; consider using secondary tablets designed to mask the iodine flavor, or adding a powdered drink mix *after* the iodine has taken effect. It's important to wait out the full treatment period before this step. If the iodine bonds with citruses in your drink mix, the treatment will be rendered ineffective—and you incapacitated.

TRAIL QUALITY

There are varying levels of wilderness in Chugach State Park. The most popular trails are fully maintained and will pose few surprises. These, however, are the exceptions. Many of the hikes in this book travel across high alpine tundra, where roving herds of Dall sheep serve as the only trail maintenance crew. Below the brush line (around 3000 feet in most parts of the park), expect dense undergrowth. Alder thrives in Southcentral Alaska, and a trail cleared last summer might be halfway overgrown this year. Some of the hikes take you into designated wilderness areas, where trails are intentionally not maintained. Traveling into completely untamed backcountry can be thrilling, but it requires fortitude and preparedness— rarely will someone else be around to offer help. Before departing, make sure you read the full hike description and know what sort of trail conditions to expect. Don't attempt a hike that exceeds your ability level. The information box at the beginning of each hike description mentions what kind of trail conditions you'll find; see the "Using This Guide" section for a description of terrain types.

SCREE AND ROCKFALL

The Chugach Mountains are composed almost entirely of loose sedimentary rock. Greywacke, known in local climbing circles as "Chugach crud," is a fragile rock that prevails throughout the park. It crumbles easily—you can snap a chunk in two with your bare hands, and it breaks just as freely from the mountainsides. If your hike takes you up any rocky slopes or gullies, look out for rockfall and consider bringing a helmet.

If you explore the Chugach Mountains for any length of time, you'll become familiar with scree slopes. Scree is a collection of small loose rocks,

A typical scree slope

large enough to cause an ankle sprain when they slip out from under you but too small to sit firmly in place. Climbing some of the peaks in this book involves traveling over scree. Sometimes, surrounding yourself with an ocean of rubble can be an eerily fascinating experience; more often it's a Sisyphean purgatory of shifting, sliding rocks, dragging you back a step for every two you take uphill. When ascending a scree slope, try to pick a path along larger rocks that will not slide as much. In scree-filled gullies, head for the edges (keeping an eye out for rockfall) where you'll find firmer rock under your feet and handholds along the gully wall.

SCRAMBLING ON CHUGACH ROCK

None of the hikes in this book require mountaineering expertise or specialized equipment. However, some involve "scrambling"—crossing moderately steep and uneven terrain, periodically using your hands for balance. Chugach rock is invariably loose and fragmentary, and all hand or footholds should be tested before being trusted. Remember that what you climb up you will most likely have to climb down, a task made more challenging by the pull of gravity, fatigue, and dehydration. Most accidents happen on descents; keep this in mind when you decide whether or not to press on to a summit. Some of the hikes in this book also require routefinding and a healthy dose of common sense. You may encounter impenetrable brush or steep drop-offs if you leave the route. Don't expect extensive trail markings except on the most popular hikes.

STREAM CROSSINGS

The Chugach backcountry is full of streams and rivers, and quite empty of bridges. You can cross many of the smaller streams without getting wet by walking or crawling across a fallen log or hopping from rock to rock. Plan the precise route of your crossing before you begin, and then proceed slowly and deliberately.

When crossing larger rivers, accept the fact that you're going to get your feet wet. Begin by scouting the river for a likely crossing place. If you need to, step back and above the river for a better view. Wider always means shallower; look for a braided area where the stream divides into two or more channels. Avoid crossing to or from steep banks, which are signs of swift and deep water. You can judge the depth of the stream by tossing rocks. A small "splash!" is promising, while a "ker-plunk!" signifies deep water to avoid. Also keep in mind that many streams in the park are fed by glaciers. As the glacier ice melts over the course of a day, what was a small stream in the morning may swell to a deluge by late afternoon. The earlier in the day you make your crossing, the better.

Once you've chosen a route, seal your cameras, stoves, and other vulnerable equipment in waterproof bags. It's a good idea to make sure you have dry clothes ready to put on at the other side. Undo your waist strap

Crossing a stream as a group can lend stability and safety. (Photo courtesy of Chugach State Park)

so you can quickly take off your pack if you fall, and loosen any gaiters or ankle-tight pants that might collect water against your clothes. Consider adding weight to your pack (rocks work nicely) if you are small; you'll benefit from the extra stability.

Ideally, cross streams in old tennis shoes or hiking sandals in order to keep your hiking boots dry. If you do not have extra footgear, remove your socks and cross in your boots. You'll be glad to have dry socks after the crossing to keep blisters at bay. *Never* cross a stream barefoot.

In swift water you should face upstream, lean into the current, and place a stick or ice ax upriver as a third point for stability. Also use your stick to probe the water depth. Two or more people can cross together, bracing one another for support. If you fall and cannot regain your footing, drop your pack and swim on your back with your head upriver and feet extended to prevent yourself from smashing into river debris, and try to work your way toward either bank. As harrowing as they sound, stream crossings can be made with relative ease if you plan carefully. Some people even call them fun.

BEARS

Bears! Few visitors enter the backcountry without the hope, at least in the back of their minds, of glimpsing an Alaskan bruin. Seeing a bear is always exciting; seeing one up close can be a little *too* exciting.

Luckily, smart hikers can almost always avoid dangerous encounters. You are a guest in the bears' home; be polite and alert them to your presence. You can ring bear bells, blow whistles, or bang pots and pans, but the most effective warning call is actually your voice. As you stumble through the brush, call out, "Hey bear! Coming through!" Or talk loudly to your hiking partners. If you're feeling musical, go ahead and break out in song. Some hikers recite poetry; Alaskan bears (traditionalists by and large) tend to prefer Shelley and Lord Byron. No matter how silly you feel shouting into the bushes, remember that bears recognize the human voice as something to avoid. If they hear you approaching, they'll almost always go away peacefully.

Bears use the same trails as you do, and are generally happy to share if you stay out of their personal space. Look for bear signs as you travel: droppings (called bear scat), tracks, and trampled grass. If you stumble across an animal carcass or see birds congregating over a food source, you might also find an angry bruin guarding its meal. If you see a lone cub, you can bet a frantic sow is nearby. In either situation, bears will be on the defensive and more disposed to attack. Leave the area immediately.

If you *do* have a close encounter of the furry kind, keep your wits about you. Bears rarely kill humans. They want trouble even less than you do and will almost always retreat if given the chance. Give them that chance! Try to back away slowly from the bear, talking to it and letting it know

Bear-bagging food along the Historic Iditarod Trail (Photo courtesy of Chugach State Park)

you're a human. If it stands on its hind legs, it's probably just trying to get a better look at you. Make yourself seem big: keep your pack on, wave your arms, and stand shoulder-to-shoulder with your hiking partner. Scold the bear sternly, but don't make any high-pitched squeals or imitate bear noises. *Do not run.* No matter how many track races you won back in high school, the bear is faster than you.

If the bear continues to approach as you back away, stop and hold your ground. Keep up your noise and arm-waving, even if it charges. Bears that charge are almost always bluffing, and will stop 10 or 20 feet in front of you. If the bear actually touches you, immediately drop and play dead. Keep your pack on, curl up in a ball, and cover your neck with your hands. Once the bear thinks you're no longer a threat it will most likely leave you alone. In rare cases, some bears (especially black bears) may think they've found a meal and will continue biting after you've stopped moving. In this case, fight back vigorously.

If you give ample warning on the trail, bears should keep out of sight; in camp, it's sometimes a different story. Avoid making camp near trails and stream banks. Set up your camp area in a triangle, with your cooking site and your food storage site both a hundred yards downwind of your campsite and a hundred yards from one another. Store *all* your food, along with trash, soap, sunscreen, toothpaste, used sanitary napkins, and anything with a strong scent in resealable plastic bags.

If possible, "bear-bag" this cache from a tree (at least 15 feet above ground, 10 feet from the trunk, and 5 feet below the branch). The easiest way to do so is to place these items into two sacks tied together with a length of string about 10 feet long. Throw one sack over an appropriate branch and use a stick or pole to push the lower sack up until the two hang at an even height. However, as much of your hiking in the park will be on the alpine tundra, you may not find an appropriate tree. As an alternative, consider sealing your cache in a bear-proof container (available from most Anchorage outfitters).

Before you go to sleep, make sure your tent and clothes are free of food scraps and garbage. Bears are dangerous, but are almost always avoidable. Following a few simple rules of hygiene and courtesy will minimize your chances of an unpleasant encounter with these elusive and magnificent creatures.

MOOSE

You may fret about bear encounters, but far more moose than bears live in Chugach State Park. Moose are peaceful herbivores, but they're also very big and sometimes grouchy. You should treat them with respect, especially if you encounter a cow with her baby. Like bears, most moose will run off if given the chance. If you find a moose blocking your path, you should yell, clap your hands loudly, and be patient. Eventually it should give way. Do not antagonize them.

INSECTS

Although the ptarmigan is officially recognized as the state bird, many Alaskans accord that honor to the mosquito. Mosquitoes don't run as thickly in Chugach State Park as they do in the Alaskan Interior, and they generally don't venture onto the higher ridges or windy areas. Still, mosquitoes, gnats, and flies are common below tree line, particularly around streams or marshes. Carry insect repellent, or apply it thoroughly before a day hike, especially during the peak mosquito season (mid-June to mid-July).

POISONOUS PLANTS

Chugach State Park is home to a diverse group of plants, most of which are benign. It does have its dangers, though. While free of poison ivy and poison oak, the park is full of devil's club, a large, leafy undergrowth with stinging spikes on both the leaves and stalk. Similarly vicious is cow parsnip, a distinctive plant with very large, three-sectioned palm-like leaves and pleasant-looking white flowers. Touch it and it will leave you with a rash. Any hike below tree line will likely pass through areas with these plants, so wearing long pants is a good idea. And while snacking on blueberries is one of the many pleasures of crossing the alpine tundra, beware of the several poisonous plants in the park: buttercups, baneberry, larkspur, water hemlock, false hellebore, and certain mushrooms. If you can't identify it, don't eat it.

HIKING WITH CHILDREN

Many of the hikes in this book are suitable for children, though the child's age, attitude, and ability will determine how far and how high he or she can enjoyably go. Younger children generally stay interested for 3 to 5 miles, though an uphill plod may reduce that distance. Some of the more strenuous hikes in this book are out-and-back trips that can be shortened to any length. Since many trailheads are close to tree line, even a short hike can take children into the playground of the high tundra. Hikes that offer interesting diversions such as lakes and waterfalls are also recommended. Be sure to keep a close eye on your children, and have them carry their own packs with water, food, extra clothing, raingear, and a whistle.

HIKING WITH YOUR DOG

Many hikers enjoy hiking with their "best friend," although it's generally better to leave pets at home. If you do bring any canine companions into the park, make sure they're as prepared as you are for unexpected events in the backcountry. Take extra food for your dogs, and make sure they drink plenty of water. Dogs are susceptible to giardia—to be safe, give them treated water only. If you will be traveling over rough terrain, bring a field harness. These can save them in a fall and also be handy for stream crossings. Most of what you carry in your first-aid kit will be useful if your

dog sustains an injury, but also add in a buffered aspirin and an extra winter booty to protect a cut or bleeding paw. Finally, keep your dog on a leash at and near the trailhead, and on all crowded trails, near wildlife, and on dangerous terrain.

HYPOTHERMIA

Hypothermia occurs when the body loses more heat than it can restore, causing a lowering of its core temperature. The park's cool, windy, and sometimes rainy summers create a constant hypothermia danger. Too many hikers charge up a mountain in short sleeves, cool off at the windy summit without adequate extra clothing, and then stumble back down in a mildly hypothermic state. It may be sweltering at the parking lot, but above tree line it's almost *never* hot.

Wet clothes and dehydration can combine to cause hypothermia even on relatively warm days. Keep an eye out for the early symptoms of hypothermia in your hiking companions: shivering, fumbling hand movements, slurred speech, irritability, and antisocial behavior. As hypothermia progresses, shivering ceases and the victim begins to lose motor control. Their pulse becomes more difficult to detect. Generally the hypothermic hiker will not recognize the problem; it's up to others to let him or her know, which often involves a certain degree of nagging to drink more water, put on more clothing, keep moving, and *stay dry*.

If someone in your party exhibits signs of hypothermia, act immediately to stop heat loss from their body. Get them out of the wind and into dry clothes. Add as many layers as possible, and have them drink hot fluids and eat high-energy foods. If possible, make them move to create internal heat. Otherwise, put them in a sleeping bag. If you have a stove, heat some water to put in bottles (stuffing the bottle in a sock so as not to burn the victim's skin) and place under the armpits and in the groin. Remember, the best way to beat hypothermia is to avoid it by keeping dry, dressed, and hydrated.

SUNBURN

Even on a cold, cloudy day, you face the risk of sunburn in Alaska's northern environment. Be especially careful if your hike crosses over snow, which strongly reflects the sun's rays. Always apply sunscreen to any exposed skin before heading out. Carry sunglasses (one of the Ten Essentials) on every hike.

WINTER HIKING

Some of the hikes in this book, due to terrain conditions and avalanche danger, are only suitable for summer use. That said, the park is a wonderful,

Baneberry, one of the park's several poisonous plants (Photo courtesy of Chugach State Park)

peaceful place to visit in winter, when it takes on an entirely different character. Many people enjoy winter travel on snowshoes and cross-country skis. If you plan on venturing into the park in the winter, check with a park ranger or park staff for snow conditions and the relative avalanche danger of your proposed route. When planning your trip, keep in mind the added rigors of winter weather and reduced daylight.

AVALANCHES

For the summer hiker, avalanches do not pose a problem. In spring, however, some slopes still covered with snow can be avalanche-prone, as can old cornices (overhanging lips of snow usually created by wind) melting in the summer sun. Always check with a ranger or park staff for current conditions before setting out. In winter, some areas of the park should be avoided due to constant avalanche danger. If you plan to travel in winter, familiarize yourself with the terrain and take a class on avalanche basics, available through The Alaska Mountain Safety Center, Inc. in Anchorage. Call (907) 345-3566 for more information.

FROSTBITE

Frostbite can strike exposed skin quickly, particularly under windy conditions. Wear or carry clothing appropriate to the worst conditions you may encounter, and stay hydrated. Your fingers, nose, ears, and toes are most susceptible. Keep them covered and warm, and keep a constant watch on your companions. If your skin starts to turn pale or white, or you begin to lose feeling in any of these areas, immediately warm the affected area with your body heat. Cup hands over your ears and nose, tuck fingers under your armpits, and warm your toes on a companion's stomach. *Never heat the areas to above body temperature (such as before a fire) or rub them even slightly.* For more severe frostbite, where the skin appears entirely white and deeply frozen, it is usually best not to attempt to thaw it in the field. A thawed limb that refreezes will be much more severely damaged than one that remains frozen. Instead evacuate the victim immediately. This is especially true for frostbitten feet: once a frozen foot has been thawed, the owner will likely not be able to walk at all and will become a severe liability to the entire party.

LEAVE NO TRACE

If not properly cared for, Chugach State Park's delicate wilderness will be quickly compromised. With hundreds of thousands of annual visitors, its trails erode quickly. Lichen trampled under a hiker's boot can take a century to recover, and campfires leave scars that last for decades. By practicing minimum impact ethics we significantly improve the health of the park's plants and wildlife. Adhere to the following guidelines on every trip:
• Pack out all trash, even biodegradable foodstuffs. Also pick up and carry out all trash you find on your hike, even if it's not yours.

- Keep your food secured at all times. This not only helps to keep the bears away, but it also prevents disruptions in the food cycle of the birds and rodents who scavenge for trail mix.
- Stick to the trail where one exists. If there is no trail, stay on rocky ground to avoid damaging fragile lichen and tundra whenever possible. Never take shortcuts across switchbacks; this is a major cause of erosion.
- Make camp in existing campsites when possible. If you do create a new campsite, visualize potential impacts upon the land. Choose one more than 100 feet away from all water sources. Do not dig any ditches, and leave flowers, rocks, and other natural features undisturbed.
- Keep your kitchen and toilet at least 200 feet away from all streams and lakes. Detergent can harm water life and degrade Anchorage's water supply, so make sure you wash your dishes well away from all water sources. Use biodegradable soap or, better still, no soap (you can wash the pot in the dishwasher at home).
- Bury all human waste in 6 inches of soil, and at least 200 feet away from streams and lakes. Do not bury toilet paper or women's sanitary products; pack them out with other trash.
- Campfires are forbidden in most of the park, and in true minimum-impact spirit, you should not build one even where they are allowed. Consider using a stove when possible. If you do need a fire, keep it within the established fire ring or on a site where a fire has previously been made. Only use "dead and down" wood, and thoroughly douse the fire with water until it is completely out.

USING THIS GUIDEBOOK

Read this section before delving into the hike write-ups themselves. It explains how to use our rating system and the hike information box that begins each hike description.

MAPS

Although to-scale maps are included with each hike in this guide, these are no substitute for a detailed topographical map showing elevation lines and terrain features. You should carry a topo map with you on every hike, especially those venturing off established trails. Each hike information block lists the United States Geological Survey (USGS) topographical map that covers the area of the hike. You can purchase many USGS maps at any outdoor store or at the Alaska Public Lands Information Center (at Fourth and F Streets, Anchorage; (907) 271-2737). The complete selection is available at the United States Geological Survey office on the Alaska Pacific University campus (4230 University Drive, Anchorage; (907) 786-7011), where you'll find topographical maps covering the entire state of Alaska, as well as the more detailed 1:25,000 scale maps that you may not be able to buy elsewhere. The USGS office can also provide maps through mail order.

At the outdoor stores you will also see a topographical map published by Alaska Road and Recreation called "Anchorage and Vicinity." This includes the area covered by all the USGS topographical maps you'll need except for the Anchorage B-7 and Anchorage B-6 quadrangles. Its trail information is usually, but not always, reliable.

A NOTE ON HIKING TIMES AND DIFFICULTY

These hikes are evaluated, both in their difficulty and the time required, for the capabilities of a reasonably fit hiker. But like the mountains, no two hikers are alike. Some of us sprint from rest stop to rest stop, while others plod slowly but surely; constant uphills easily demoralize some hikers, but others wait breathlessly for the view over the next rise. Before you rush into one of the trips in this book, think about *your* hiking style. If you're unfamiliar with the park, start with an easier hike. Note how long it takes you to complete and how difficult *you* think it is, and calibrate your experience against our ratings. We have done our best to keep these ratings consistent, so you can adjust them to your own sense of hiking time and difficulty. Keep in mind that a slower, steadier pace is safer and more efficient, and that hiking faster or climbing higher than you are capable of safely doing is an invitation for mishap.

Always have a topographical map—
and know how to read it.

THE HIKE INFORMATION BLOCK

This information, located at the top of every hike description, provides a summary of the hike. With a quick glance you'll be able to evaluate the hike's length, difficulty, and special features. Many hikes have multiple destinations, and one information block is included for each.

Distance gives the total mileage for the recommended route, listed as the round trip distance from the trailhead unless otherwise noted. Some hikes are best done as traversals from one trailhead to another (such as the popular Crow Pass Crossing), and in these instances the distance is for one way only. Some hikes on established trails lack a definitive turnaround point, and in these cases we list the range of possible distances.

Elevation Gain is the total vertical distance climbed on the hike. Due to the ups and downs of the terrain, this sometimes may be significantly more than the difference between the starting elevation and the high point.

Hiking Time is the range of time a reasonably fit hiker will need to complete the hike. Long day trips will be given in hours, but could also be divided into 2 or more days.

Hike Difficulty has very little to do with the brute exertion required to complete the hike. (You can estimate that yourself by looking at the distance and elevation gain.) Rather, this is a subjective measure of less obvious factors that may complicate the hike. Read the full hike description for more insight into the factors behind a hike's rating. The hikes are grouped into the following four levels:

An "easy" hike will be straightforward, usually on a maintained or obvious trail, without any dangers or difficulties.

A "moderate" hike may require small bits of scrambling or steep terrain, or may require you to venture slightly off the beaten path.

A "moderate to difficult" rating denotes slightly harder or more sustained terrain challenges, and may also reflect isolation or greater exertion.

A "difficult" rating reflects significant exertion, multiple stretches of sustained challenging terrain, possible bushwhacking, routefinding challenges, isolation, and possible rockfall danger or other objective hazards.

Terrain signifies the dominant or most difficult types of terrain covered by the hike. The hikes are divided into the following categories, in generally ascending order of difficulty:

An "established trail" is relatively clear and easy to follow, though not necessarily marked or signposted. Above tree line this may be a well-worn path across the tundra.

A "rough trail" is unmarked and patchy, and it may occasionally disappear. Irregularly maintained at best, the trail may become overgrown.

"Alpine tundra" is open terrain above tree line with relatively easy walking. This will often have a trail or obvious route, but may require routefinding in poor visibility.

Wilderness in our backyard: the isolated North Fork of Ship Creek seen from Paradise Pass

"Scree" warns of shifting, uneven rocky ground, such as that found in a mountain gully or a glacial moraine.

"Scrambling" signifies steeper mountain slopes, generally rocky, which require the use of hands to traverse. In mountaineering terms, this would be considered Class 3 climbing with possibly some exposure.

"Backcountry" is found below tree line, with no appreciable trail, dense undergrowth, and/or rough terrain. Routefinding skills are essential.

High Point indicates the highest elevation reached on the hike.

USGS Maps indicates which USGS topographical quadrangle(s) cover the hike area. See the above section on maps for more information on the USGS topos.

EXPLORING OFF THE BEATEN PATH

By no means restrict yourself to the routes recommended in this book. Even though we have attempted to discuss every walkable trail and most non-technical peaks, it would be impossible to outline the web of routes formed by all of these trails and destinations. With this book and a topo map, you can easily see how paths may link in ways we have not discussed. Heed this book's warnings and stay within your capabilities, but remember that this guidebook is only a beginning. Explore the park on your own terms.

THE NORTH PARK

Bordered by Knik Arm and massive Knik Glacier, the northern region of Chugach State Park abounds with rugged wilderness and high peaks. It's a mountaineer's playground, with many awe-inspiring peaks too difficult to surmount without the proper equipment and expertise. Most striking are Kiliak and Yukla in Eagle River Valley, The Mitre and East Twin Peak near Eklutna, and the higher "Symphonic Peaks"—Calliope, Flute, and Organ—around Eagle Lake.

Still, there's no shortage of challenging but walkable terrain. Test your scrambling skills on Eagle Peak and Cantata Peak, or explore isolated alpine valleys in the Ewe Valley backcountry and Hanging Valley. There are plenty of enticing lowland trails, too. Follow a mile-long footpath to Thunder Bird Falls, immerse yourself in wooded solitude on the Ptarmigan Valley Trail, or explore Eklutna Lake's extensive system of well-maintained trails.

The north park receives comparatively less rain, resulting in thinner foliage and a slightly lower tree line. The weather here is generally a little kinder—on a rainy August day, head to Eklutna or Pioneer Ridge and you might find a reprieve from the downpour.

While there is plenty of alpine tundra spread throughout Chugach State Park, in the north park you'll find particularly inviting walks along alpine ridges, such as Mount Magnificent Ridge and the hike to Blacktail Rocks. In the lowlands are wide valleys filled with wildlife, especially Eagle River Valley. A must-see for every visitor is the Eagle River Nature Center, where you can learn about the plants, animals, and geology of the area. And after a day-long hike up the Historic Iditarod Trail, you can cool your heels in Eagle River near its source. Coming directly from Eagle Glacier, it is probably the coldest water you'll ever dip a toe in.

Pioneer Peak (Photo courtesy of Chugach State Park)

1 PIONEER RIDGE AND SOUTH SUMMIT

Upper Pioneer Ridge
Distance: 9 miles
Elevation Gain: 5200 feet
Hiking Time: 7 to 9 hours
Hike Difficulty: moderate
Terrain: established trail
High Point: 5330 feet
USGS Map: Anchorage B-6

Pioneer Peak, South Summit
Distance: 12 miles (round trip from Pioneer Ridge Trailhead)
Elevation Gain: 6400 feet
Hiking Time: 8 to 12 hours
Hike Difficulty: moderate to difficult
Terrain: scrambling
High Point: 6350 feet
USGS Map: Anchorage B-6

On a clear summer day, no outing can compare with a hike up Pioneer Peak. This quintessential Chugach trek climbs through a dense forest to rolling alpine tundra and spectacular vistas. Yet Pioneer Peak is also unique, a high peak rising with alarming abruptness from the muddy banks of Knik Arm. Few mountains have such a dramatic profile—and fewer still are so pleasant to climb. A well-maintained trail, stopping just short of Pioneer's summit, makes the miles zip by. Above tree line you'll find three improbably placed picnic tables, so pack a lunch and snack in style while admiring Knik Glacier and the distant white peaks of the high Chugach Mountains. Ambitious scramblers can cap off a wonderful day in the sun by continuing to Pioneer Peak's craggy south summit, a good scramble past the trail's end.

Getting There: Pioneer Ridge Trailhead. Drive north from Anchorage on the Glenn Highway for 25 miles. Take the Old Glenn Highway exit, which comes immediately before the main highway crosses Knik River. Follow this paved but bumpy road for 9 miles to the intersection with Knik River Road. No sign marks this intersection; look for it as the Old Glenn Highway begins to curve left before crossing Knik River. Rather than follow the curve, continue straight. The trailhead lies 4 miles further, marked by an elegant wooden sign on the right side of the road. The sign is set back a little into the brush, so pay attention or you might pass it without noticing.

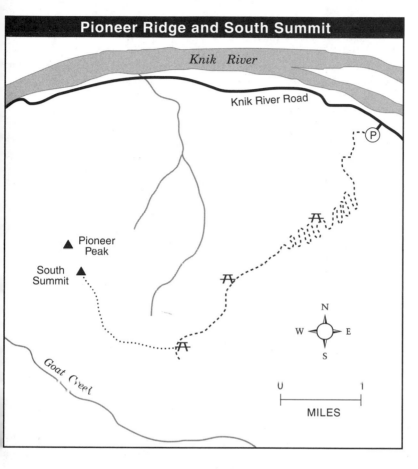

The trail starts climbing immediately from the trailhead and rarely relents from its steady uphill chug. Wooden boards cross several muddy sections, and parts of the trail may be overgrown with devil's club and alder. After climbing for about 2 miles, the trail emerges from the trees onto grassy slopes. No water is available beyond this point, so make sure to fill up at one of the streams below tree line. The first of the three picnic tables— carried up in pieces by the Colony High School Junior Reserve Officer Training Corps—sits right at tree line. Lounge for a minute and enjoy views across Matanuska Valley and the Palmer Hay Flats. The first table is a suitable turnaround point if you're short on time or energy.

After a series of steep switchbacks, the trail gains the crest of Pioneer Ridge and flattens out somewhat near mile 3. With the hardest part now behind you, take a good look at the mighty surrounding peaks. Most prominent is Mount Marcus Baker, at 13,176 feet the highest mountain in the entire Chugach Range, rising to the east above immense Knik Glacier.

Orange stakes mark the trail above tree line, although the route simply follows the ridge and should be obvious. The trail descends briefly and then climbs a small rise. To the right of the trail, just below this rise (near mile 4), lies the second picnic table, sitting at an elevation of 4300 feet. From here, the trail continues up a long, final hill to a broad plateau. This marks the end of the trail proper, and is where you'll find the third table—surely the most scenic site for a picnic table ever devised. Hike south for 200 yards to a lookout point with views of Bold Peak, Bashful Peak (named for the way it just peeks out from behind massive Bold Peak, which dominates the horizon), and Eklutna Glacier. At 8005 feet, Bashful is the highest mountain in Chugach State Park, though it's dwarfed by the snow-capped behemoths near Knik Glacier.

Most hikers will turn around at the third picnic table, but experienced scramblers can press on another 1½ miles and 1000 vertical feet to the south summit of Pioneer Peak. Continue along the ridge, following a sheep trail westward to a small saddle below the summit ridge. Here the route steepens. Stay on the ridge crest whenever possible, and traverse to the right (north) around difficult sections. This is a classic Chugach scramble— watch your step and look out for loose rock.

Pioneer's south summit is 4 feet lower than its northern peak, but don't try to cross the notch between the two summits without proper mountaineering equipment—and even then think twice. Four feet notwithstanding, the view from South Pioneer Peak can't be beat, taking in the high Chugach, massive Denali and its neighbors, and the distant volcanoes of western Alaska.

Knik Glacier and Knik River, from Pioneer Ridge

Unless, of course, it's cloudy. And it's often cloudy.

But don't take it too hard: that's part of hiking in Alaska. Carefully retrace your steps to the third picnic table and follow the orange markers leading back down to the trailhead.

2 | EKLUTNA LAKESIDE TRAIL

Distance: 2 to 26 miles
Elevation Gain: 300 feet
Hiking Time: varies with distance
Hike Difficulty: easy
Terrain: established trail
High Point: 1200 feet
USGS Map: Anchorage B-6

When it established Chugach State Park in 1970, the Alaska Legislature insisted the new park's lands and waters remain open to diverse uses. This is certainly the case with Eklutna Lake: in addition to being an outdoor mecca, it generates a substantial share of Anchorage's electricity and provides the city with 35 million gallons of drinking water each day. Yet Eklutna—a gray-blue arc of a lake surrounded by sharp peaks—remains unspoiled. A typical summer day sees families strolling along the lakeshore, hikers heading for the alpine tundra at East Twin Pass, backpackers setting up tents at two campgrounds along the Lakeside Trail, boaters enjoying calm water along the lake's 7-mile length, and mountaineers setting off on the demanding 30-mile Whiteout Glacier traverse to Girdwood. Eklutna takes these sundry visitors in stride, with room enough for all. The area's main thoroughfare is the Eklutna Lakeside Trail, which runs 13 miles from the lake's western shore to the doorstep of Eklutna Glacier. It provides access to several farther-flung trails, and also makes for a pleasant outing in its own right.

Getting There: Eklutna Lake Trailhead. Drive north out of Anchorage on the Glenn Highway. Take the Eklutna exit at mile 26. From the exit ramp, signs direct you to make two quick right turns onto a frontage road. Shortly down this road, another sign points you left onto Eklutna Lake Road. This road runs 10 miles to the lake (only the first 2 miles are paved), passing a toll booth and a ranger station before reaching the lake facilities. Expect to pay a fee for day parking and camping at the drive-in sites at the trailhead (but the campsites along the Lakeside Trail are free).

The Eklutna Lakeside Trail, a dirt road built by the U.S. military for training operations, winds through mixed forests, skirting the northern shore of Eklutna Lake. This road is in excellent shape, with fewer potholes

Eklutna Lakeside Trail and Bold Ridge Overlook

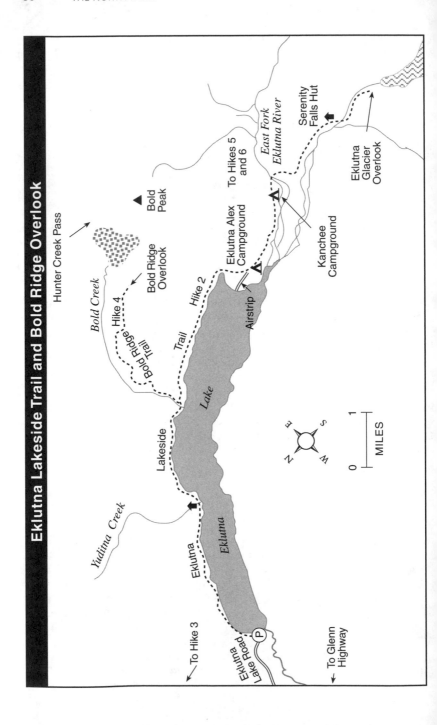

than some Anchorage streets. Yet thanks to the lack of automobiles (banned since 1977), tranquillity prevails. The trail has recently been smoothed and widened, and at times splits into upper (newer) and lower (older) routes. The lower sections, although rougher, are preferred by hikers for their gentler grades and scenic lake vistas; they're off-limits to motorized vehicles during the summer. On the upper sections, all-terrain vehicles are allowed from Sunday through Wednesday.

A walk on the Lakeside Trail can be as lengthy or brief as you like. Less than a mile from the parking lot lie several excellent lakeside picnic spots. Most hikers will want to make an out-and-back day trip, perhaps biking part of the distance in order to quickly reach the upper valley (bikes are available for rent at the trailhead and can be stashed in the woods relatively securely). Others will want to stay overnight and make several outings. With some advance planning, you can rent the elegant Yuditna cabin at mile 3, or a section of the Serenity Falls public-use hut near the end of the trail at mile 12. (Reserve either cabin in person or by mail at the Department of Natural Resources Public Information Center, 550 West Seventh Avenue, Twelfth Floor, Anchorage, AK 99501. You can check on availability by calling the Public Information Center at (907) 269-8400 or on the Internet at *www.dnr.state.ak.us*.) Otherwise, you'll find two pleasant campgrounds at miles 8 (Eklutna Alex Campground, named after the last shaman at Eklutna village) and 10 (called Kanchee, the Dena'ina word for "porcupine") with fire pits, picnic tables, and outhouses.

Eklutna Lake from the Lakeside Trail

The Lakeside Trail follows the lake's northern and eastern shores for 7 miles, then continues up the valley. A popular trail to Bold Ridge Overlook (Hike 4) departs from the Lakeside Trail at mile 5. Shortly past Kanchee Campground, the trail intersects the East Fork Eklutna River Trail (Hike 5), which also offers access to Bold Peak (Hike 6).

The Lakeside Trail crosses Eklutna's eastern tributary on a sturdy bridge just after the turnoff for the East Fork Trail (mile 10½). Past the bridge, it continues into the upper Eklutna Valley beneath the fabulously misnamed Benign Peak and sheer-walled The Mitre. It ends after 13 miles at the forlorn Eklutna Glacier Overlook, marked by a small sign and—curiously—no glacier whatsoever. The glacier retreated out of view shortly after the overlook was built, leaving the site with the air of a ghost town.

Nevertheless, the glacier overlook is worth a visit. Pay heed to potential rockfall and follow the trail to its end, traversing a winding ribbon of land sandwiched between high rock faces and a torrential glacial stream. Here, hidden behind a bottleneck of wet, cold rock, a small valley is emerging inch by inch as Eklutna Glacier retreats. Only lichens, small shrubs, and alder (Alaska's hardiest tree) have colonized this virgin ground. You can feel the temperature drop as you enter this narrow valley, where glacial melt water surges by, only inches away from your feet. Don't step too close to the river, as the banks are constantly eroding and shifting.

The broken trail peters out near an old state park interpretive display, where the frigid, thunderous water prevents further progress. Before leaving, however, listen for a moment to the rush of the river; it's the sound of centuries-old snow cascading toward Eklutna Lake, ultimately to reach the Pacific Ocean—perhaps with a detour through the faucets of modern-day Alaska.

3 | TWIN PEAKS TRAIL

East Twin Pass
Distance: 7 miles
Elevation Gain: 3500 feet
Hiking Time: 6 to 8 hours
Hike Difficulty: moderate
Terrain: established trail, alpine tundra
High Point: 4450 feet
USGS Map: Anchorage B-6

This well-maintained trail climbs above Eklutna Lake to East Twin Pass, where Dall sheep roam by the dozens. A dirt road carved out of the hillside by the U.S. Army and eventually abandoned, the Twin Peaks Trail was used only by sheep hunters for many years. Now it's an accessible and popular

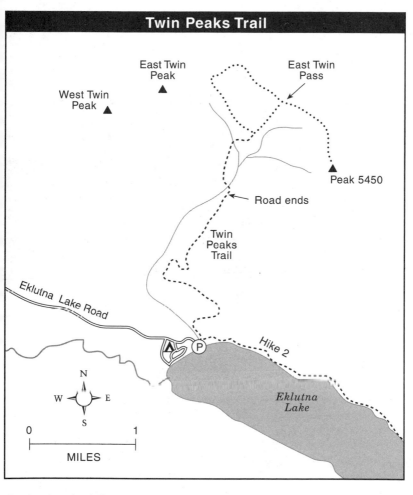

Twin Peaks Trail

East Twin
Peak ▲

West Twin
Peak ▲

East Twin
Pass

▲ Peak 5450

← Road ends

Twin
Peaks
Trail

Eklutna Lake Road

Hike 2

Eklutna
Lake

N
W ← → E
S

0   1
MILES

destination for hikers. Walk to the road's end at tree line, continue on a loop past East Twin Pass to the base of the Twin Peaks, or climb to a high lookout point above the lake. With a gentle grade leading through trees and tundra, and dramatic vistas of Eklutna Lake and close-up views of imposing East Twin Peak, the Twin Peaks Trail has something for everyone.

Getting There: Eklutna Lake Trailhead. Drive north out of Anchorage on the Glenn Highway. Take the Eklutna exit at mile 26. From the exit ramp, signs direct you to make two quick right turns onto a frontage road. Shortly down this road, another sign points you left onto Eklutna Lake Road. This road runs 10 miles to the lake (only the first 2 miles are paved), passing a toll booth and a ranger station before reaching the lake facilities.

East Twin Peak seen from East Twin Pass

From the day-use parking lot, cross a small footbridge, bear left onto the Twin Peaks Trail, and start climbing. The old roadbed switches back several times through birch and spruce. After about 1½ miles, at a prominent switchback, the vegetation opens to reveal a picture-perfect view of Eklutna Lake and massive Bold Peak. This view alone makes the trip worthwhile. Consider hiking here during a summer evening to watch a spectacular sunset over the lake; the wide and clear trail allows a safe hike down in twilight.

Beyond the viewpoint, the trail turns northward and climbs more steeply. Soon you enter the upper valley, where the eroding slopes of East Twin Peak vividly offset the grace and symmetry of Eklutna Lake. Although the Twin Peaks are among the ugliest mountains in the park, they're somehow compelling. Made of a crumbling, fragmentary rock called greywacke, they seem to be on the verge of implosion. East Twin is not only ugly, but also dangerous—at least one hiker has died from a fall after becoming lost on its steep slopes. There is no easy way to the summit; don't attempt to climb this peak unless you are properly trained and equipped.

The roadbed continues to wind uphill in the shadow of East Twin Peak until it dead-ends after 2½ miles, just above tree line. From here, look for a footpath descending to the left. It continues across a creek and climbs the tundra slopes to the northeast, then peters out on the barren slopes below East Twin Pass. Continue to the pass, where you'll find views north across Matanuska Valley and the town of Palmer. Keep an eye out for Dall sheep in the valleys north of the pass: they gather here in great numbers.

To complete the loop, turn left and follow the ridge west for 1 mile, over a high point and down to a second saddle. Here, at the base of a jagged ridge rising precipitously to the summit of East Twin Peak, turn left and descend grassy slopes to the southeast. Look for the narrow trail you ascended earlier and follow it back down through the valley floor to the roadbed.

If you want to climb a mountain, avoid the Twin Peaks and instead head up Peak 5450. Turn right at East Twin Pass and continue southeast along the ridge for 1 mile. Gentle terrain leads to the summit, where you'll find more spectacular views of Eklutna Lake and skyscraping mountains to the north.

4 | BOLD RIDGE OVERLOOK

Distance: 17 miles (7 miles round trip from Lakeside Trail)
Elevation Gain: 3700 feet
Hiking Time: 5 to 6 hours (from Lakeside Trail)
Hike Difficulty: moderate
Terrain: established trail, alpine tundra
High Point: 4456 feet
USGS Map: Anchorage B-6

Climbing through mixed forests and idyllic alpine meadows, the Bold Ridge Trail is hard to beat for scenery both above and below treeline. The trail follows an abandoned roadbed through a canopy of birch and alder to treeline, then enters a large cirque at the base of Bold Peak's striking north face. A short climb up the tundra to Bold Ridge rewards you with an expansive view of Eklutna Lake, distant Knik Arm, and Eklutna Glacier.

Getting There: Eklutna Lake Trailhead. Drive north out of Anchorage on the Glenn Highway. Take the Eklutna exit at mile 26. From the exit ramp, signs direct you to make two quick right turns onto a frontage road. Shortly down this road, another sign points you left onto Eklutna Lake Road. This road runs 10 miles to the lake (only the first 2 miles are paved), passing a toll booth and a ranger station before reaching the lake facilities.

To reach the Bold Ridge Overlook Trail, you must first travel the initial 5 miles of the Eklutna Lakeside Trail (Hike 2), a wide gravel road following the shoreline. Biking this stretch (bikes are available for rent at the trailhead) of the Lakeside Trail will save you several hours and allow for a leisurely day trip. Look for a sign marking the Bold Ridge Overlook Trail just past the bridge over Bold Creek.

The trail, wide and clear, climbs consistently but gradually. After 1½ miles it reaches a subalpine meadow, then curves broadly south into the upper U-shaped valley, a huge glacially carved bowl beneath Bold Peak.

Sunset over Eklutna Lake, from Bold Ridge Overlook

From here the ramparts of Bold Peak come fully into view, a steep maze of chutes and gullies funneling rock onto the valley floor. You'll also see evidence of glacial action in the peculiar arcing waves of rock and dirt covering the upper valley. These huge mounds, reminiscent of an abandoned construction site, testify to the immense power of ice to mold mountains.

After climbing slightly above the U-valley floor, the old roadbed suddenly ends. This will mark a turnaround point for some hikers, but the best views are still to come. Follow a sheep trail leading up to the ridge on your right. Once you've attained the ridge crest, head southeast to Bold Ridge Overlook (point 4456), about ¼ mile away. High above crescent-shaped Eklutna Lake, you'll be able to survey the entire Eklutna Valley, from the lower river to the glacier and massive ice fields beyond. Past the overlook, the ridge climbs steeply to Bold Peak's summit. Do not continue further on this ridge, which soon turns dangerously steep; instead see Hike 6 for a much easier route up Bold Peak.

You can also extend your hike by exploring the upper Bold Valley, still scarred by centuries of glaciation. Clamber over the jumbled terrain to the base of Bold Peak, or head directly across the valley to Hunter Creek Pass. Beyond this pass lies the seldom-visited Hunter Creek drainage, one of the wildest areas of the park.

5 | EAST FORK EKLUTNA RIVER TRAIL

Tulchina Falls
Distance: 26 miles (5 miles round trip from Lakeside Trail)
Elevation Gain: 300 feet
Hiking Time: 2 to 4 hours (from Lakeside Trail)
Hike Difficulty: moderate
Terrain: established trail
High Point: 1300 feet
USGS Map: Anchorage B-6

Upper East Fork Valley
Distance: 36 miles (15 miles round trip from Lakeside Trail)
Elevation Gain: 900 feet
Hiking Time: 8 hours or more (from Lakeside Trail)
Hike Difficulty: moderate to difficult
Terrain: rough trail, backcountry
High Point: 1900 feet
USGS Maps: Anchorage B-6, Anchorage A-6

This small trail branches from the Eklutna Lakeside Trail, winds along Eklutna River's eastern tributary, and leads past spectacular Tulchina Falls to the gateway of a backcountry wilderness. It's best hiked as a day outing from Eklutna Alex or Kanchee Campgrounds (located at miles 8 and 10 of Lakeside Trail), though if you bike the Lakeside Trail you can easily make it a day trip from the trailhead. Adventurous hikers may want to press on past trail's end and explore the upper East Fork Valley.

Getting There: Eklutna Lake Trailhead. Drive north out of Anchorage on the Glenn Highway. Take the Eklutna exit at mile 26. From the exit ramp, signs direct you to make two quick right turns onto a frontage road. Shortly down this road, another sign points you left onto Eklutna Lake Road. This road runs 10 miles to the lake (only the first 2 miles are paved), passing a ranger station and a toll booth before reaching the lake facilities.

Follow the Lakeside Trail on foot or on bike (available for rent at the trailhead) for 10½ miles. The East Fork Trail branches off from the Lakeside Trail just before a major bridge crossing East Fork Eklutna River.

The trail is thin but generally easy to follow. Logs bridge all river crossings. The first mile, scratched into the steep hillsides of Bold Peak, is rocky and uneven, but as you continue upvalley the trail flattens amid mixed forests. Tall birch and spruce drop welcome shade across the trail, and the murmuring rush of Eklutna River's East Fork provides a steady reminder of your seclusion.

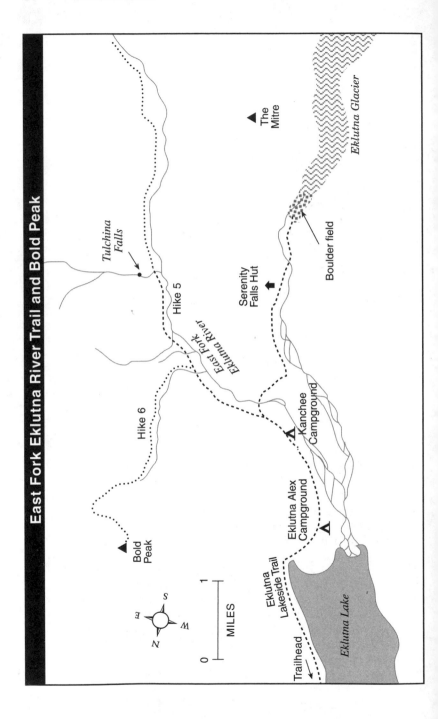

East Fork Eklutna River Trail and Bold Peak

Eklutna Glacier

The Mitre

Tulchina Falls

Boulder field

Serenity Falls Hut

Hike 5

East Fork Eklutna River

Hike 6

Kanchee Campground

Bold Peak

Eklutna Alex Campground

Eklutna Lakeside Trail

Trailhead

Eklutna Lake

S
E — W
N

MILES

0   1

The East Fork of Eklutna River

After 2½ miles you'll reach a sign marking Tulchina Falls. The upper falls, best seen from the trail, are impressive enough, but for an even better view, turn left and follow a gravel bar to the foot of the lower falls, which crash upon a shelf and rebound in a graceful sweep before tumbling to your lookout spot. The gravel bar also makes for a good camping spot, with readily available water and close views of The Mitre's sheer eastern cliffs.

The trail continues with lesser degrees of maintenance and markings for another 5 miles through the upper valley. Here the marked trail ends and the underbrush thins, inviting off-trail exploration. Travel may be difficult below the brush line, but several clear side valleys beckon higher up. If you venture deep enough into the valley, you'll even glimpse the icy fingers of Whiteout Glacier. Bring a topographical map and your sense of adventure.

6 | BOLD PEAK

Distance: 29 miles (8 miles round trip from Eklutna Lakeside Trail)
Elevation Gain: 6600 feet
Hiking Time: 1 to 2 days
Hike Difficulty: difficult
Terrain: rough trail, scrambling, alpine tundra, scree
High Point: 7522 feet
USGS Map: Anchorage B-6

Bold Peak dominates the Eklutna Lake skyline, rising more than 6500 feet from Eklutna's shores in an explosion of steep rock walls and scree. However, this peak is easier to climb than it looks. Although the cliffs along Bold's lakeside face prevent a frontal assault, you can sneak up on the mountain when it is not looking: a long, hidden gully winds leisurely up the mountain's backside. This gully, tucked so deep into the mountain that it practically swallows you, makes for a unique Chugach climb. It's 12 miles from the Eklutna Lake parking lot to the base of this gully, so only the fastest hikers (even with the aid of a bicycle) will want to attempt a 1-day ascent. Plan instead on staying overnight at one of the Lakeside Trail campgrounds or at the Serenity Falls hut and devoting 2 days to this outing. Bold Peak is not for everyone: it's a long climb that involves routefinding, some difficult scrambling, and plenty of tiring scree, but also pleasant hiking and unbeatable views.

Getting There: Eklutna Lake Trailhead. Drive north out of Anchorage on the Glenn Highway. Take the Eklutna exit at mile 26. From the exit ramp, signs direct you to make two quick right turns onto a frontage road. Shortly down this road, another sign points you left onto Eklutna Lake Road. This road runs 10 miles to the lake (only the first 2 miles are paved), passing a ranger station and a toll booth before reaching the lake facilities.

Follow the Eklutna Lakeside Trail for 10½ miles to the East Fork Eklutna

River Trail. Biking to this point saves several hours, but from here you'll have to proceed on foot.

The beginning of the East Fork Trail (Hike 5) is rough and may be washed out in places. After about 1 mile, the trail crosses a tributary stream that drains a large gully to your left. This has been named Stivers Gully after Bill Stivers, a former member of the Mountaineering Club of Alaska who pioneered this route. To reach the base of the gully, turn left (north) at the stream crossing and bushwhack up the tributary's banks. You may find yourself hopping from one side to the other in search of better walking, but take heart: this is the worst terrain of the entire climb, and it only lasts for ¼ mile.

Once in the narrow and steep-walled gully, you'll find a long, uphill plod over scree and talus—consider bringing trekking poles, an ice axe, or a walking stick for added balance on these shifting rocks. The edges of the gully may offer better footing, but watch for rockfall. Higher up, the gully forks. Follow the right branch (the left branch quickly turns vertical). You may see an old fixed rope dangling off the cliffs higher in the right fork. Don't trust your weight to it (who knows how many winters it has weathered?), but it indicates that you're heading the right way. The gully steepens above the fork, then opens up for a short section of exposed scrambling where the rope is fixed. This section can be difficult for inexperienced scramblers, especially on the descent; keep this in mind when deciding whether or not to continue.

The rugged East Fork Eklutna River Valley, seen from Bold Peak

At the top of this pitch, you'll emerge from the gully into a high alpine valley. You may spot a sheep trail winding across the hillside: do not mistake this for the route. Climb a little higher and traverse left, above a series of eroded gullies, onto a small but prominent bench. Look for cairns marking the way.

From the bench, continue traversing northeast through a boulder field and up into a high cirque. Snow may persist here until late summer. Continue climbing to the obvious saddle at the upper end of the cirque. Atop the saddle, turn left and ascend the scree slopes to the northwest, aiming for a row of three rocky outcroppings straight ahead. Continue above the outcroppings up to the summit ridge; from here it's an easy jaunt northward to Bold's broad, rocky summit. Good luck trying to figure out which point is the actual summit—several knobs vie for that title, and at last check the summit register was missing. From here, a mile above Eklutna Lake, you can peer over vast ice fields to the east—certainly one of the more spectacular views in the park. Just hope clouds don't sock you in! Descend as you came, taking care to locate the top of Stivers Gully, which can be easy to miss on the way down.

7 | THUNDER BIRD FALLS

Distance: 2 miles
Elevation Gain: 200 feet
Hiking Time: ½ to 1½ hours
Hike Difficulty: easy
Terrain: established trail
High Point: 300 feet
USGS Map: Anchorage B-7

Though it's one of the shortest walks in Chugach State Park, the Thunder Bird Falls Trail reaches into a wonderful part of Anchorage's backyard wilderness. The trail winds through tall birch and cottonwoods to a sturdy deck with a vantage over Thunder Bird Falls, and a side spur leads down to the banks of Thunder Bird Creek. Chugach State Park owns only 10 acres around the falls; the neighboring land has been ceded to the Athabascan natives living in nearby Eklutna village. They once hunted and fished throughout this area, and have regained some ownership rights since the 1968 Alaska Native Claims Settlement Act. The woods remain as quiet and still as they were centuries ago, before European ships ever charted Alaska's shores.

Thunder Bird Falls

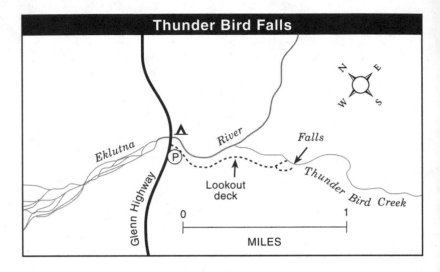

Thunder Bird Falls

Getting There: Thunder Bird Falls Trailhead. From Anchorage, head north on the Glenn Highway for 25 miles to the Thunder Bird Falls exit. Follow the exit road for ¼ mile to the well-developed trailhead. It is on the right, just before Eklutna River. You'll find plentiful parking, outhouses, and picnic benches.

The trail, wide and level, leads southeast through a predominantly birch forest. Private homes line the right edge of the trail, and a steep gorge drops to your left. After ½ mile, you'll reach a small lookout deck perched high above the surging glacial meltwaters of Eklutna River Gorge. With views of craggy East and West Twin Peaks, the deck is an inviting stop.

From the deck, continue on the trail another ½ mile to a marked fork. The thunderous falls soon come within earshot; follow the right fork for an equally impressive visual, or turn left for a less spectacular but serene river walk. It is less than ¼ mile to either destination, so you can easily visit both on the same trip.

The right fork crosses a sturdy boardwalk leading to a second lookout deck, with views of the tumbling waterfall. Stay on the trail, if not for safety's sake then to avoid the devil's club blanketing the hillside. Consider visiting on a mid-winter day, when you'll see the falls frozen into a slowly shifting sculpture of ice.

The left fork heads downhill, reaching Thunder Bird Creek after several switchbacks. It then continues upstream to the falls. You can't quite see the falls from here, but don't try to climb the slippery hillside for a better view. While this is an excellent trip for children, keep a watchful eye on them near the swift creek.

8 MOUNT EKLUTNA AND BEAR MOUNTAIN

Mount Eklutna
Distance: 5½ miles
Elevation Gain: 2700 feet
Hiking Time: 3 to 5 hours
Hike Difficulty: moderate
Terrain: established trail, alpine tundra
High Point: 4110 feet
USGS Map: Anchorage B-7

Bear Mountain
Distance: 3 miles
Elevation Gain: 1700 feet
Hiking Time: 3 to 4 hours
Hike Difficulty: moderate
Terrain: established trail, rough trail
High Point: 3160 feet
USGS Map: Anchorage B-7

Mount Eklutna and Bear Mountain, tiered hills above the town of Peters Creek, sit at the tip of a ridge stretching from the heart of the park like emissaries to civilization. Neither mountain is heavily traveled, yet both are easily reached. The Mount Eklutna Trail meanders through a lupine-filled meadow, then climbs a sculpted ridge to the summit. Bear Mountain is a shorter but less pleasant hike, steep and eroded in some sections. Nevertheless, it sees a steady trickle of locals eager to visit the peak towering so dramatically above their community.

Getting There: Peters Creek Trailhead. Follow the Glenn Highway north from Anchorage. About 17 miles after Muldoon Road, take the Peters Creek exit, turning right onto Ski Road. After about a mile, turn right on Whaley. Stay on Whaley as it becomes Chugach Park Road, then turn left on Kullberg. Follow Kullberg through several switchbacks and then turn right onto Malcolm Drive. After about ¼ mile, just before the road bears left, you will see the trailhead straight ahead of you. Park in the cleared space along the right side of the road.

Walk past a gate and onto the Peters Creek Trail, an old roadbed. Hikers heading up Mount Eklutna should follow this trail for about 2 miles. As you come over a rise, you'll see a large mountain directly ahead of you. Once this is in view, look for a trail heading left into the woods. Follow this trail through a corridor of alders and into a meadowed copse of birch and

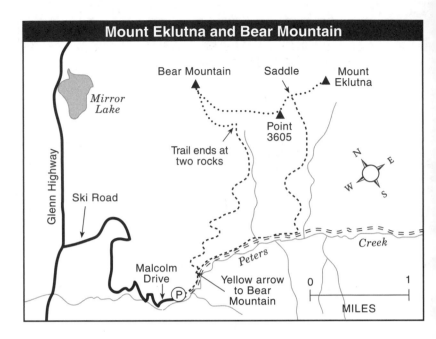

Mount Eklutna and Bear Mountain

Bear Mountain

Saddle

Mount Eklutna

Mirror Lake

Point 3605

Trail ends at two rocks

Glenn Highway

Ski Road

Malcolm Drive

(P)

Yellow arrow to Bear Mountain

Peters

Creek

0   1

MILES

hemlock. Intimate but not overgrown, this charming trail might tempt even adamant peak-baggers to linger below tree line.

After a mile the trail climbs out of the brush and then levels at the base of a steep climb to the summit ridge. Follow the obvious trail up the gully in front of you to a narrow saddle. Here the trail peters out. Ascend the wide ridge to your right. Once you've attained the high point above the saddle, continue along the ridge over several small rises to the summit, a modest bump marked by a cairn. Enthusiastic ridge-walkers can press on past Eklutna's summit for another 13 miles, all the way to distant Thunder Bird Peak. (Doing so requires at least 2 days for the round trip.)

To climb straight to Bear Mountain from the trailhead, follow the Peters Creek Trail for ¼ mile. As it crests a hill and curves down to the left, look for a birch tree on your left, marked with a faded yellow arrow. The Bear Mountain Trail begins here. The trail picks its way through a forest and then climbs into dense brush. Watch for mud and roots at your feet and devil's club dangling in your face. Above the woods, the trail turns steeply uphill and follows a gully all the way to the summit ridge. Take care when descending; the trail becomes very slippery when muddy.

After rising out of the gully onto a broad, gentle ridge, the trail passes between two large rocks and abruptly ends. From here, veer left and make your way across tussocks to the summit directly north. Finding your way back to these two rocks from the summit area may be difficult. Make a mental note of your route for the descent.

Devil's club, bane of hikers

A slightly longer loop connects Bear Mountain and Mount Eklutna via a high traverse. From Bear Mountain, head east up a gentle slope, beautifully terraced in bands of lichen and bare gravel, to an obvious high point. Descend east to a small saddle. From here you can climb over Point 3605 or traverse north of it, via a sheep trail cutting across a sea of yellow lichen, to a second saddle. From this saddle, make the short jaunt to Eklutna's summit or simply head south down the Mount Eklutna Trail and back to the trailhead. The complete loop past both peaks takes about 4 to 6 hours.

9 | PTARMIGAN VALLEY TRAIL

Distance: 2 to 8 miles
Elevation Gain: 200 to 2300 feet
Hiking Time: 1 to 6 hours
Hike Difficulty: easy
Terrain: established trail, rough trail
High Point: 2500 feet
USGS Map: Anchorage B-7

Though mostly a land of open tundra and jagged mountains, Chugach State Park also boasts acres of verdant forests. You'll find these in spades on the

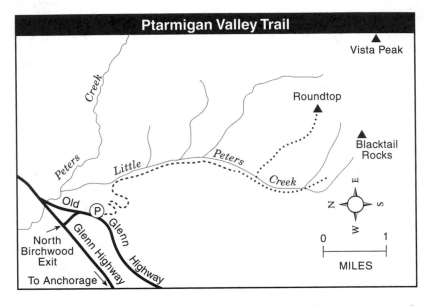

Ptarmigan Valley Trail, a gentle walk through a boreal forest teeming with moose, porcupine, wolverines, jays, warblers, and a multitude of other winged and four-legged creatures. Designed for snowmobilers, the trail is kept wide and free of brush. After winding along a hillside for about 4 miles, it enters the upper Ptarmigan Valley (also called Little Peters Creek Valley), where you can hop onto a high ridge if you want a view. The true charm of this trail, however, lies in the woods themselves—dark, dense, and vibrant.

Getting There: Ptarmigan Valley Trailhead. Follow the Glenn Highway north from Anchorage for 16 miles to the North Birchwood exit. Head east for ¼ mile on Birch Loop Road, then turn right onto the Old Glenn Highway. Follow this for just over ½ mile and turn left into a gravel parking lot. Look for state park signs marking the turn. Two lots provide ample parking, though the upper lot is usually open only during winter.

The Ptarmigan Valley Trail enters the trees immediately from the upper parking lot and meanders extensively before heading uphill into the Little Peters Creek drainage. The trail leads up small rises and curves back down the hillside, gaining elevation gradually. Keep an eye out for two common dangers: moose and devil's club. The latter, a large leafy shrub, has sharp needles on its leaves and stem.

After about 1½ miles, the trail diverts onto a smaller path and gains a small rise before dropping into Ptarmigan Valley proper. Here it joins an older, wider trail, formerly a homesteader's road. Bend right and follow this trail along Little Peters Creek to its headwaters. Trail quality diminishes in the upper valley, though the track remains easy to follow.

The trail reaches tree line high in Ptarmigan Valley, about 4 miles from the trailhead. Once above tree line you can climb a ridge leading to the summit of Roundtop, at 4755 feet. Turn left off the trail and head east through low brush to the base of Roundtop's northwestern ridge. You won't find any trail markings, so bring a map and keep track of your location. From Roundtop's nondescript summit, you can continue southeast along the ridge toward Vista Peak or to Blacktail Rocks (see Hike 10); otherwise, retrace your steps.

The Ptarmigan Valley Trail

10 BALDY AND BLACKTAIL ROCKS

Baldy
Distance: 2 miles
Elevation Gain: 1300 feet
Hiking Time: 1 to 3 hours
Hike Difficulty: easy
Terrain: established trail
High Point: 3038 feet
USGS Map: Anchorage B-7

Blacktail Rocks
Distance: 7 miles
Elevation Gain: 2700 feet
Hiking Time: 4 to 6 hours
Hike Difficulty: moderate
Terrain: rough trail, alpine tundra
High Point: 4446 feet
USGS Map: Anchorage B-7

In the foothills above Eagle River is a bare, rounded knob unofficially known as "Baldy." Less than a mile from Meadow Creek Trailhead, and with slightly more than 1000 feet of elevation to climb, it is a popular day hike with locals of all ability levels. Baldy also marks the beginning of a long, pleasant ridge leading to Blacktail Rocks and beyond. The trail is smooth, the ridge wide, and the views outstanding.

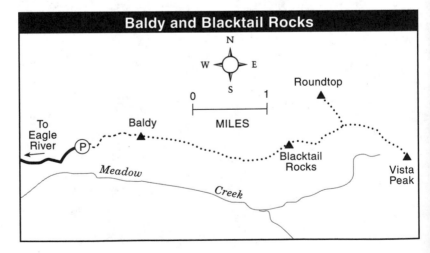

Looking west toward Blacktail Rocks

Getting There: Meadow Creek Trailhead. From Anchorage, head north on the Glenn Highway to the Eagle River Loop/Hiland Drive exit. Follow Eagle River Loop Road for about 3½ miles, and then turn right on West Skyline. The road switches back several times and changes names (from West Skyline to Jamie, McCrary, Upper Skyline, Canyon View, and finally Golden Eagle); stick to the main paved road. The pavement ends at a gated private drive; do not proceed beyond this point. There is a pullout in front of the gate with plenty of room for parking.

Proceed on foot up the small dirt path leading directly uphill from the trailhead (do not follow the private road). The rounded dirt summit of Baldy is clearly visible. The dirt path soon forks near a radio tower at the end of a gravel road. Follow the left fork. Shortly thereafter the trail forks again. Go left and proceed to a third fork. There head right, and begin climbing in earnest. Now above tree line, the heavily used trail branches out across the hillside. Stick to the main path to minimize further erosion.

The summit of Baldy, at the crest of this rise, makes a nice rest stop and lookout point. It is a great hike for a summer evening, providing an easy route and quick views. Many people stop here, but the views ahead only improve.

Continuing past Baldy, the ridge flattens and widens. Cross a wide blueberry-filled meadow and admire the ramp suddenly rising toward Blacktail Rocks. The easy walking continues until you are ½ mile from, and 1100 feet below, Blacktail Rocks; then the trail swings uphill and the climbing resumes. As you near the top, you'll see a series of rock outcroppings. Follow a faint trail slightly off the ridge, cut in front of the smaller outcroppings, and curve up from behind the northernmost rock to reach the high point.

Vin Hoeman named Blacktail Rocks after the dark lichen eking out an existence on the mountain's southern cliffs. There is some confusion as to which of the outcroppings is the highest—the furthest rocky pinnacle on the ridge seems to be the true high point, but the summit register has been placed one rock south. No matter; the rocks are (for the most part) not overly steep and fun to explore. Before you return to the trailhead, hike

¼ mile farther along the ridge to a high point for an impressive view of these black-and-gray capped cliffs rising from the green valley below.

Now that you've gained all this elevation, why not reward yourself with some easy ridge-walking? Continue northeast along the gently undulating ridge to its junction with another ridge running northwest and southeast. A left turn will take you to the nondescript point named Roundtop; turn right to reach Vista Peak, 1½ miles farther along the ridge. The going is easy until just below Vista's summit, where you may want to traverse onto the peak's south side to avoid a short section of scrambling. Not many hikers continue past Vista, but it is possible to follow the ridge all the way to Mount Significant (11½ miles one way from the trailhead) and beyond—perhaps even to the rarely visited Ram Valley (16 miles one way from the trailhead), a beautiful place to pitch a tent or spend a clear night beneath the stars.

11 | MOUNT MAGNIFICENT AND MOUNT SIGNIFICANT

Mount Magnificent
Distance: 5 miles
Elevation Gain: 2300 feet
Hiking Time: 4 to 5 hours
Hike Difficulty: moderate
Terrain: established trail, alpine tundra
High Point: 4285 feet
USGS Map: Anchorage B-7

Mount Significant
Distance: 14 miles
Elevation Gain: 5200 feet
Hiking Time: 7 to 10 hours
Hike Difficulty: moderate to difficult
Terrain: alpine tundra
High Point: 5400 feet
USGS Map: Anchorage B-7

Homes and roads pile atop one another throughout the lower Eagle River Valley, pushing ever higher up the hillsides. Above this sprawl, however, is one of the most scenic ridge walks in Chugach State Park. An unbroken string of gentle peaks extends the length of Eagle River Valley, beckoning walkers of all abilities. The hardest part of the hike is finding the pint-sized trailhead. It's tucked halfway up the hillside, only minutes from downtown Eagle River.

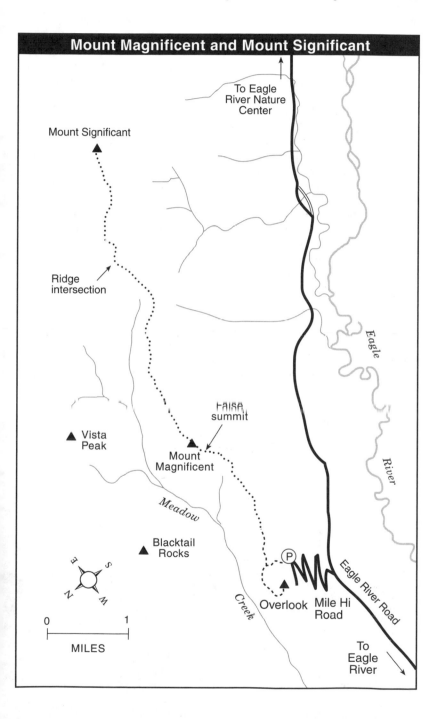

Mount Magnificent and Mount Significant

To Eagle River Nature Center

Mount Significant

Ridge intersection

Vista Peak

False summit

Mount Magnificent

Meadow

Blacktail Rocks

N E S W

Eagle River

P

Overlook

Mile Hi Road

Creek

Eagle River Road

To Eagle River

0 1

MILES

Getting There: Mile Hi Pass Trailhead. From downtown Anchorage, drive north on the Glenn Highway. Take the Hiland Drive exit at mile 10. Bear right off the exit ramp and continue through the traffic light on Eagle River Loop Road. After 2½ miles, at a major intersection, turn right onto Eagle River Road. Drive another 2 miles to a Y intersection; turn left here onto Mile Hi Road. This steep road repeatedly changes names as it climbs; follow the obvious uphill switchbacks to where the pavement ends. Look for a small turnout just before a sign reading, "No parking beyond this point." The turnout, marked by a second sign indicating the Chugach State Park boundary, is the trailhead.

From the road, a steep and narrow path leads uphill into the woods. It soon runs underneath the powerlines, then intersects an old roadbed; turn right and follow the road ¼ mile to Mile Hi Pass. From the pass, you can climb to an overlook point above Eagle River or continue east to Mounts Magnificent and Significant.

To reach the overlook point, simply continue on the old road over Mile Hi Pass as it climbs the hill to your left (west). After ½ mile, the road ends atop a rounded high point, with excellent views of Eagle River and the Alaska Range.

A longer hike leads east to Mount Magnificent, so named after seven years of lobbying by a local woman. When the U.S. Senate Committee on Place Names refused her request on the grounds that such a meager mountain did not merit so superlative a name, she took the matter to the Alaska Legislature—and won! To evaluate the mountain's claim to magnificence firsthand, turn right off the old roadbed at Mile Hi Pass and follow a narrow trail uphill. This track eventually peters out in the tundra; try to keep to the rocks along the ridge line to avoid trampling fragile vegetation.

Ridgewalking on the way to Mount Magnificent

Follow the ridge over two prominent high points, then head northeast across a high valley floor and up grassy slopes to a false summit. From here, stay slightly north of the ridge line until directly below the true summit to avoid a short section of scrambling. At the summit you'll find magnificent views and a pile of rocks housing the summit register.

It's another 4½ miles along the ridge to Mount Significant, so named for being significantly taller than little Mount Magnificent. This is arguably the most pleasant ridge walk in the park. On a sunny day, you can admire the web of valleys and streams beneath you. On cloudy days the ridge is sealed off from the world below, intimate and peaceful. In limited visibility, though, it's easy to accidentally start down a side ridge and get off course—bring a compass and know how to use it.

Follow Dall sheep trails over Mount Magnificent and down to a wide saddle. Continue southeast and east over several rises, about 3 miles, until you intersect a roughly perpendicular ridge. Here you can head northwest to Vista Peak and Blacktail Rocks (see Hike 10), a long and ambitious loop. To reach Mount Significant, continue southeast over the next high point and down to a saddle, then up a long, final ridge. The grassy summit reveals a fascinating contrast: south lies the populated Eagle River Valley, while to the north is pristine Peters Creek Valley and its barren peaks. It is a fitting place to ponder the significant advantages of having a wilderness in one's backyard.

Lying just east of Mount Significant is spectacular Ram Valley. Unfortunately, the valley is not publicly accessible from Eagle River Road, so if you wish to enter it (or hike out after descending from Mount Significant) you must contact private landowners for permission to cross their land. Otherwise, retrace your steps along the winding ridge to Mile Hi Pass.

12 | EAGLE RIVER TRAILS

Distance: ¾ to 8 miles
Elevation Gain: 0 to 300 feet
Hiking Time: ½ to 5 hours, or overnight
Hike Difficulty: easy
Terrain: established trail
High Point: varies
USGS Maps: Anchorage A-6, Anchorage A-7

Alaskan explorer Walter Mendenhall once called Eagle River Valley "a miniature Yosemite," and every year more than 50,000 visitors find out why. In addition to stunningly sheer valley walls, these visitors find a wealth of gentle, wooded trails and the Eagle River Nature Center. The

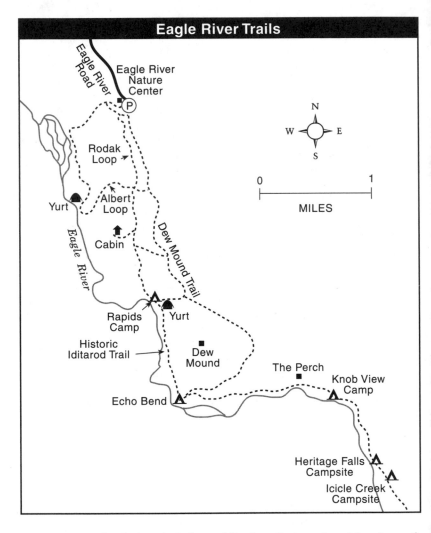

Eagle River Trails

Eagle River Road

Eagle River Nature Center

P

Rodak Loop

Yurt

Albert Loop

Eagle River

Cabin

Dew Mound Trail

N
W — E
S

0   1

MILES

Rapids Camp   Yurt

Historic Iditarod Trail

Dew Mound

The Perch

Knob View Camp

Echo Bend

Heritage Falls Campsite

Icicle Creek Campsite

nature center, funded entirely by public donations and parking fees, offers natural history exhibits and educational programs such as guided
nature walks, lectures, and children's events. On any given day you might
take part in a wild mushroom hunt, watch beavers build a dam and king
salmon spawn, attend an astronomy program, or learn how to make
syrup from birch sap. The nearby trails boast almost as much variety as
the nature center itself. Within a few minutes' walk of the center are a
salmon viewing deck, a self-guided geology tour, and the banks of Eagle
River. Longer walks lead farther up the valley, where a public-use cabin

and two yurts (teepee-like domed tents constructed over wooden plat-forms and equipped with stoves) are available for nightly rent. Check the nature center's program schedule or reserve the cabin and yurts online at *www.ernc.org*.

Getting There: The Eagle River Nature Center. From downtown Anchorage, drive north on the Glenn Highway. Take the Hiland Drive exit at mile 10. Bear right off the exit ramp, proceed through a stoplight, and continue straight on Eagle River Loop Road. After 2½ miles, at a major intersection, turn right onto Eagle River Road. Follow it for 11 miles to its end at the nature center. There is a $5 parking fee, which is not covered by the Alaska State Parks annual pass.

Several trails begin at the nature center, ranging from the short Rodak Loop to the 26-mile Historic Iditarod Trail (described in full as Hike 45). They all overlap to some degree, but for the sake of clarity each one is described separately.

Rodak Loop: This flat, wheelchair-accessible, ¾-mile loop travels through riparian habitat to a salmon viewing deck and a beaver dam. It's a good hike for young children, or for a quick jaunt in the woods after participating in one of the nature center's programs.

Albert Loop: The Albert Loop winds from the nature center down to Eagle River's gravel bars and back, a total of 3 miles. It's the best trail in the area for access to the river and has a signposted tour of the local geology. Learn how glaciers form and witness their impact upon the landscape firsthand. (The tour is self-guided, but a brochure available from the nature center explains the sights at each signpost.) A short side trail leads to the Eagle River just below the nature center for a unique camping experience. A section of the Albert Loop Trail is closed seasonally during the salmon run (usually July 15 through the end of September) to let the bears feed in peace.

Dew Mound Trail: For a longer walk, head down the main path from the nature center a short distance and then veer left onto the Dew Mound Trail. Built in 1999, it runs parallel to and just north of the Iditarod Trail; branches connect the two trails at several points. The trail leads through quiet stands of birch and spruce and around Dew Mound (an impressive glacial erratic) before reaching Eagle River at Echo Bend. Turn right here to complete the 7-mile loop. Several marked trails lead back to the Iditarod Trail before Dew Mound, allowing you to shorten the loop to your liking.

Historic Iditarod Trail: This is the big one, running 26 miles from the Eagle River Nature Center to Girdwood. It's an immensely popular trip, although most backpackers begin in Girdwood and finish at the nature center 2 or 3 days later. The nature center end of the trail is ideal for day hikes, however. Hike to Echo Bend (6 miles round trip) or The Perch (8 miles round trip) for jaw-dropping views of Mount Yukla. There are also

Polar Bear Peak as seen from the Rodak Loop Trail

five designated campsites within 6 miles of the nature center, great for overnight out-and-back trips. Go upscale and reserve the public-use cabin, or be adventurous and camp on one of Eagle River's many gravel bars. Wherever you spend the night, remember that this valley is home to a sizable black bear population—bear-bag your food or store it away from your campsite in a bear-proof container. Learn how to do this, and all about bears and the other inhabitants of the valley, at the nature center before you go.

13 | RIVER WOODS TRAIL AND SOUTH FORK FALLS

Distance: 4 miles (one way)
Elevation Gain: 100 feet
Hiking Time: 1½ to 3 hours
Hike Difficulty: easy
Terrain: established trail
High Point: 350 feet
USGS Map: Anchorage B-7

On this lovely riverside trail, just minutes from suburban Eagle River, you can amble in the woods, see Eagle River's swirling confluence with its South Fork, and visit a spectacular waterfall. The River Woods Trail, true to its name, winds through deciduous forest along South Fork Eagle River to the main fork of Eagle River, then follows the river downstream almost to the Glenn Highway. It's a great place to hike with children, go for a run, or collect autumn leaves.

You can access the trail from either end, at South Fork Falls or the Eagle River boat launch facility. The Eagle River boat launch has toilets, better parking, and a resident park host to answer questions. The South Fork Falls end is off the beaten path and lacks a designated parking area, but brings you to within ¼ mile of the impressive South Fork Falls.

Getting There: River Woods Trailhead: Take the Glenn Highway north from Anchorage for 10 miles and exit at Hiland Drive. To reach the South Fork Falls end of the trail, turn right from the exit ramp onto Hiland Drive

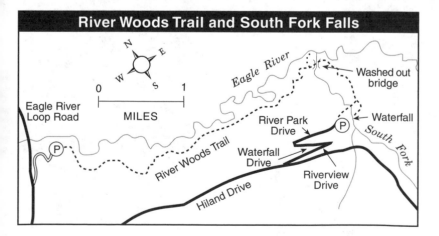

and continue for 3¼ miles to Riverview Drive. Turn left on Riverview, and then left onto Waterfall Drive (the continuation of the paved road). Follow Waterfall to River Park Drive, turn right, and follow this road for about ½ mile. River Park Drive dead-ends at a gate, where the hike begins. Park on the side of road, but do not block the gate.

To reach the Eagle River boat launch, follow the Glenn Highway to the Hiland Drive exit, then continue on Eagle River Loop Road through the stoplight at Hiland Drive. Follow Eagle River Loop Road for ½ mile, then turn right onto a dirt road just before the bridge across Eagle River. The parking area is on your left just past the turn. Expect to pay a $5 parking fee.

From South Fork Falls Trailhead, continue on foot down River Park Drive past the gate. Please respect the privacy of nearby homeowners. Stroll down the curving dirt road, cross the bridge over the creek, and turn right at the intersection onto another dirt road. After several minutes of walking, turn right off this road onto a wide track, which leads several hundred feet east toward a viewing area overlooking South Fork Falls.

If you'd like to continue on the River Woods Trail, retrace your steps to the first intersection and go straight. Follow the wide dirt road for about ½ mile to the South Fork crossing. In the summer of 2000, the bridge

The South Fork Falls

spanning the South Fork was washed out, so you'll need to ford the creek—not difficult but somewhat chilly—should you wish to hike the full distance.

If you start from the Eagle River boat launch, look for trailhead signs leading to a boardwalk. The wide trail meanders alongside Eagle River through willow, alder, and birch. Periodic views of Mount Magnificent and neighboring peaks create a sense of space, making this one of the more pleasant walks below tree line in the Anchorage area. After about 3 miles you'll reach the South Fork confluence, where swift glacial waters and gravel bars marked by occasional bear tracks add a touch of of wildness.

The South Fork ford site is just south of the confluence. Continue to the ford site and complete the hike (you'll need to arrange a car shuttle or pickup), or turn around and return to the boat launch trailhead.

14 | EAGLE LAKE AND LOOKOUT POINT

Eagle Lake
Distance: 10 miles
Elevation Gain: 800 feet
Hiking Time: 5 to 6 hours
Hike Difficulty: easy
Terrain: established trail
High Point: 2700 feet
USGS Maps: Anchorage A-7, Anchorage B-7

Lookout Point
Distance: 12 miles
Elevation Gain: 1800 feet
Hiking Time: 6 to 8 hours
Hike Difficulty: moderate
Terrain: rough trail, alpine tundra
High Point: 3600 feet
USGS Maps: Anchorage A-7, Anchorage B-7

Five miles up South Fork Eagle River lie silty-green Eagle Lake and its brilliant blue twin, Symphony Lake. These two lakes, one fed by glacial runoff and the other by rain and snowmelt, pose a vivid contrast best seen from a lookout point 900 feet above their shimmering waters. You can reach the lakes on a gentle trail worn by day hikers; a short climb up bare slopes past the trail's end reaches the lookout. This hike is easily done in a day, but Eagle Lake also makes a good base for exploring more distant reaches of the park.

Getting There: South Fork Eagle River Valley Trailhead. From

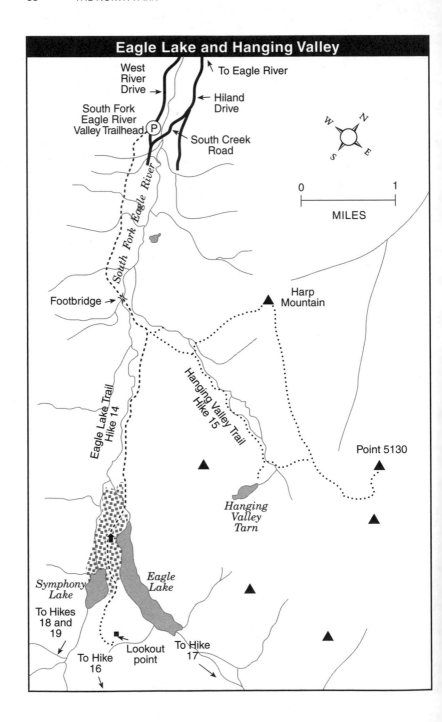

Eagle Lake and Hanging Valley

West River Drive

To Eagle River

Hiland Drive

South Fork Eagle River Valley Trailhead

P

South Creek Road

South Fork Eagle River

0 — 1

MILES

Footbridge

Harp Mountain

Eagle Lake Trail Hike 14

Hanging Valley Trail Hike 15

Point 5130

Hanging Valley Tarn

Symphony Lake

Eagle Lake

To Hikes 18 and 19

To Hike 16

Lookout point

To Hike 17

Anchorage, head north on the Glenn Highway for 10 miles and take the Eagle River Loop/Hiland Drive exit. Turn right off the exit ramp, and then right again at the first stoplight onto Hiland Drive. Follow Hiland for several miles, cross a bridge over South Fork Eagle River, and turn right onto South Creek Road. Follow this for a short distance and then make a sharp right onto West River Drive. The trailhead and a dirt parking lot are on the left, just past the turn.

The Eagle Lake Trail follows a wooden boardwalk into the woods, flitting in and out of spruce trees as it climbs to a bench above the river. Two miles from the trailhead, it plunges back into the valley and crosses Eagle River on a sturdy bridge.

Across the bridge, the trail turns muddy at times. You'll soon come to a sign marking a small fork. To the left (though not named on the sign) is Hanging Valley (Hike 15). The main trail continues to the right and heads straight up the valley, gradually climbing through sporadic brush and stunted trees. Glacial debris carpets the valley floor, blending into a landscape of moraine rubble near Eagle Lake.

Across the boulder field, the trail follows a thin moraine dividing Eagle Lake from Symphony Lake. This glacial deposit, long since recovered by

A hiker rests above Eagle and Symphony Lakes.

vegetation, offers excellent views of both lakes and the surrounding peaks, making it a perfect stopover for lunch. An odd, octagon-shaped hut sits nearby, constructed decades ago by a homesteader hoping to claim the land around Eagle Lake as his own. While an eyesore, this hut can provide adequate shelter in a pinch. If you plan on camping out, though, you're better off making your own campsite along Eagle Lake's south shores.

To continue to the lookout point, follow the main trail past the octagon-shaped hut. Climb the large hillside just southeast of Symphony Lake, where the trail peters out. Continue up a gully dividing two high points—a large rocky outcropping to your right, and a smaller knob on your left. The knob on the left is your goal.

For an overnight outing, camp at the lakes and explore deeper into the park. Visit two pristine tarns above Symphony Lake (Hike 18) or a retreating glacier (Hike 17), climb a challenging peak (Hike 16), or trek into a remote alpine valley (Hike 19) where Dall sheep graze.

15 | HANGING VALLEY TRAIL

Hanging Valley Tarn
Distance: 10 miles
Elevation Gain: 1700 feet
Hiking Time: 5 to 6 hours
Hike Difficulty: easy
Terrain: established trail, alpine tundra
High Point: 3350 feet
USGS Maps: Anchorage A-7, Anchorage B-7

Point 5130
Distance: 12 miles
Elevation Gain: 3400 feet
Hiking Time: 6 to 8 hours
Hike Difficulty: moderate
Terrain: established trail, alpine tundra
High Point: 5130 feet
USGS Maps: Anchorage A-7, Anchorage B-7

Off the main trail to Eagle Lake lies Hanging Valley, named for its striking geologic origin. A hanging valley is created when a glacier retreats up a large valley (in this case South Fork Eagle River), leaving smaller side valleys still filled with glacial tongues. As these smaller glaciers retreat, they leave U-shaped valleys with floors higher than that of the main valley. The smaller valleys therefore appear to "hang" halfway up the sides of a larger valley. Chugach State Park boasts many such hanging valleys, but few are as accessible as this one. An easy trail leads through the valley to an isolated tarn and climbs to a high point on the valley wall. Such a quiet and beautiful place, so near a trailhead, is a rarity.

Getting There: South Fork Eagle River Valley Trailhead. From Anchorage, head north on the Glenn Highway for 10 miles and take the Eagle River Loop/Hiland Drive exit. Turn right off the exit ramp, and then right again at the first stoplight onto Hiland Drive. Follow Hiland for several miles, cross a bridge over South Fork Eagle River, and turn right onto South Creek Road. Follow this for a short distance and then make a sharp right onto West River Drive. The trailhead and a dirt parking lot are on the left, just past the turn.

From the trailhead, follow the main trail toward Eagle Lake. After 2 miles, the trail crosses South Fork Eagle River on a footbridge, then forks. The right fork leads to Eagle Lake; take the smaller left fork to reach Hanging Valley. About 100 feet later the trail forks again; turn right and climb a short rise into Hanging Valley. Many game trails crisscross the valley floor, petering out among rocks higher in the valley. Try to stay on the main trail (which parallels the south bank of the creek) to minimize erosion. Expect some muddy patches in spring.

A hike in Hanging Valley can take a few hours or all day, depending on

Clouds hanging low over the Hanging Valley

your time and energy. Consider two main destinations: a secluded tarn nestled in a cirque near the valley's end, or a sloping peak, set back and above the valley.

To reach Hanging Valley Tarn, continue up the valley for about 2 miles. Pass a small lake and continue to a stream tumbling down the slope to your right (south). Hike directly up the tundra just to the right of this stream to reach the tarn several hundred feet above. Debris-strewn mountain walls tower a thousand feet above the cobalt lake, which may remain frozen and buried in snow well into summer. Sporadic patches of grass and lichen— and perhaps a family of ducks on the water—are the only signs of life.

The second destination, Point 5130, rises from the opposite side of Hanging Valley. From the valley floor (below the tarn), head straight north up a steep, grassy slope to a prominent saddle. At this saddle, turn right (east) and ascend a broad ridge to a flat area below Point 5130. From here, veer left (north) and climb another 600 feet to the summit. On a clear day, you'll have vistas over the entire Eagle River Valley.

If you want to explore further, visit Harp Mountain, a broad triangular peak near the valley's mouth. Climb as described above to the saddle above the Hanging Valley floor. Then, instead of turning right and hiking to Point 5130, turn left and ascend the ridge to the northwest. Climb 2 miles along the ridge on gentle tundra punctuated by short rocky sections to reach Harp's summit. From here, the wide Susitna Flats and the eternally white Alaska Range are visible. Descend as you came, or hike down the steep gully heading south from the summit—a rougher but more direct route. Cross the valley floor through light brush to the main trail.

16 | CANTATA PEAK

Distance: 17 miles (7 miles round trip from the hut at Eagle Lake)
Elevation Gain: 4600 feet
Hiking Time: 10 to 13 hours (5 to 7 hours from the hut at Eagle Lake)
Hike Difficulty: difficult
Terrain: alpine tundra, scree, scrambling
High Point: 6410 feet
USGS Maps: Anchorage A-7, Anchorage B-7

Cantata Peak, one of the more imposing mountains in Chugach State Park, is not an easy climb. It involves a long approach hike, some difficult scrambling, and extensive routefinding. For competent and experienced Chugach scramblers, though, it's a rewarding trip. Cantata can be climbed in a day

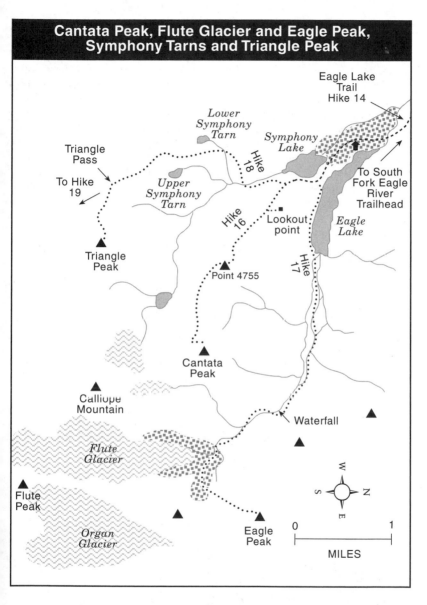

Cantata Peak, Flute Glacier and Eagle Peak, Symphony Tarns and Triangle Peak

Eagle Lake Trail Hike 14

Lower Symphony Tarn

Symphony Lake

Triangle Pass

To Hike 19

Upper Symphony Tarn

Hike 18

To South Fork Eagle River Trailhead

Hike 16

Lookout point

Eagle Lake

Triangle Peak

Point 4755

Hike 17

Cantata Peak

Calliope Mountain

Waterfall

Flute Glacier

Flute Peak

Eagle Peak

Organ Glacier

0   1
MILES

from South Fork Trailhead, though routefinding challenges on the upper mountain make it sensible to start early. Most hikers will prefer to camp near Eagle Lake and devote 2 days to the climb.

Getting There: South Fork Eagle River Valley Trailhead. From Anchorage, head north on the Glenn Highway for 10 miles and take the Eagle

River Loop/Hiland Drive exit. Turn right off the exit ramp, and then right again at the first stoplight onto Hiland Drive. Follow Hiland for several miles, cross a bridge over South Fork Eagle River, and turn right onto South Creek Road. Follow this for a short distance and then make a sharp right onto West River Drive. The trailhead and a dirt parking lot are on the left, just past the turn.

Follow the Eagle Lake Trail for 5 miles to Eagle Lake. From the moraine dividing Eagle and Symphony Lakes, continue along a small trail to the eastern shores of Symphony Lake. Ascend the slopes southeast of Symphony Lake to a broad flat bench and continue up the massive gully leading southeast. This grand staircase, climbing 1500 feet in a graceful curve, is a natural wonder. There is no trail but the walking is easy. Stick to the gully's center and climb straight toward the low saddle just north (left) of Point 4755.

Cantata's summit pinnacle can be seen from this saddle. Take a good look at the route before pressing onward, as it is easy and potentially dangerous to get lost in the maze of small gullies high on the mountain. Look for a prominent notch about two-thirds of the way up the western ridge. This is a key landmark—here you'll be forced to abandon the ridge and cut across the mountain's southern slopes.

Next proceed east, past Point 4755, to the base of Cantata's western ridge. Here the real climbing begins. Follow the ridge closely, diverting only when necessary to scramble around overly steep sections. Several cairns mark the route, but they may be hard to spot. Stay close to the ridge line and you should find a manageable way up. Be prepared to use your hands; this is classic Chugach scrambling.

After climbing about 1000 feet, you'll reach the large notch in the ridge. A giant cairn marks this point, and it should be obvious that you can't continue past the vertical faces blocking further progress along the ridge.

Cantata Peak, seen from the Symphony Tarns

Carefully descend into the notch and traverse directly east across the mountain's south face. Maintain a consistent elevation and cross a series of at least five gullies. After about ¼ mile, you'll reach wide-open scree slopes. Here turn uphill and return to the summit ridge.

Once you've regained the ridge, it's a short and pleasant walk to the summit. Thousands of feet below to the east, icy-blue Flute Glacier lies cradled by sheer mountain walls. These neighboring mountains, especially fierce Calliope to the southeast, seem to crowd Cantata's summit and lend it an alternately desolate and intimate character.

As you descend, be careful to exactly retrace your traverse through the gullies to the all-important notch. (On the ascent, consider building a cairn or leaving a piece of brightly colored cloth where you exited the gullies to help you return to the same point on your way down.) Back at the base of the west ridge, you'll marvel at where your own two feet (with a little help from your hands) have carried you.

17 | FLUTE GLACIER AND EAGLE PEAK

Flute Glacier Overlook
Distance: 18 miles (8 miles round trip from the hut at Eagle Lake)
Elevation Gain: 2500 feet
Hiking Time: 10 to 13 hours (5 to 7 hours from the hut at Eagle Lake)
Hike Difficulty: moderate to difficult
Terrain: rough trail, scree, backcountry
High Point: 5400 feet
USGS Maps: Anchorage A-7, Anchorage B-7

Eagle Peak
Distance: 20 miles (10 miles round trip from the hut at Eagle Lake)
Elevation Gain: 5300 feet
Hiking Time: 13 to 17 hours (8 to 11 hours from the hut at Eagle Lake)
Hike Difficulty: difficult
Terrain: scree, scrambling
High Point: 6955 feet
USGS Maps: Anchorage A-7, Anchorage B-7

Despite their proximity to popular Eagle Lake, the windswept glacial erratics, lichen fields, and meltwater rivulets of Flute Glacier Valley see few human visitors. Hikers exploring the 4-mile length of this valley will find easy walking, abundant room for camping, and the chance to walk right up to the base of a massive glacier. The truly adventurous might also find their way up Eagle Peak, a challenging scramble. While it's possible to reach both Flute Glacier and Eagle Peak in 1 long day from South Fork Trailhead, most people will want to make this an overnight trip and camp out on Eagle Lake's shores or halfway up Flute Glacier Valley.

Getting There: South Fork Eagle River Valley Trailhead. From Anchorage, head north on the Glenn Highway for 10 miles and take the Eagle River Loop/Hiland Drive exit. Turn right off the exit ramp, and then right again at the first stoplight onto Hiland Drive. Follow Hiland for several miles, cross a bridge over South Fork Eagle River, and turn right onto South Creek Road. Follow this for a short distance and then make a sharp right onto West River Drive. The trailhead and a dirt parking lot are on the left, just past the turn.

Follow the well-maintained Eagle Lake Trail for 5 miles to Eagle Lake. From here, head east along the lake's south shore, toward Flute Glacier Valley. Small game trails line the lakeshore but disappear at its eastern edge. After a short section of bushwhacking and stream hopping, you'll reach the wide gravel bars of the valley floor just above Eagle Lake.

Follow the gravel bars east, weaving through low trees. Numerous bear, moose, and wolf tracks may hint at the easiest path—but keep an eye out for these valley dwellers! Step carefully from one gravel bar to the next and you might keep your feet dry, but more likely you'll have to splash through at least one glacial rivulet. Ford sites are easy to find, as are camping spots on the gravel bars. After following the river for 1½ miles, you'll come to a steep waterfall. Keep to the north bank of the river and approach the scree slopes slightly left of the waterfall. Expect a brief stretch of bushwhacking, and pick your way up these scree slopes toward the upper valley. Once you're level with the top of the waterfall, return to the riverbank just above the falls.

Ahead lies the upper Flute Glacier Valley, only recently uncovered by the glacier's retreat. Flute Glacier is hidden from view, but its chill fills the air. Continue up the valley floor on whichever side of the stream offers the best footing. You'll want to end up on the north bank of the stream before approaching a short rise higher in the valley. At this rise, look for a trail cut into the slopes just north of the stream. Follow it up to a gray, scree-strewn plateau overlooking Flute Glacier—this makes a good campsite, surrounded by the sounds of creaking glacial ice and distant, tumbling rocks. Explore the area around the glacier's snout, but don't venture onto the ice without proper training and equipment.

While Flute Glacier will mark the end of the trip for most hikers, expert scramblers might want to continue to the summit of Eagle Peak. This involves gaining 2400 vertical feet in just over ½ mile—no easy task. Eagle is

Flute Glacier, one of Eagle River's sources

a "walk-up," not requiring any mountaineering equipment, but the steepness and difficulty of the route make it off-limits to novices. Reaching the summit requires good judgment, plenty of routefinding, and a wealth of perseverance. You'll also need decent weather, as wet rock makes for dangerous scrambling. Snow patches lingering on the route make this a poor choice for an early season climb.

From the snout of Flute Glacier, head due east into a high cirque. Ascend a scree field leading to the base of a large gully spilling down Eagle's south face. At the top of this field, a small stream pours down a short section of steep rock. This section requires some difficult scrambling and is a good test: if you are not comfortable with the climbing here, don't continue. However, the climbing above is no more difficult, so if this short bit of scrambling is within your abilities, you should be able to handle this hike.

While the scrambling doesn't get any tougher, the routefinding certainly does. There are no trail markings and the twisting route defies detailed description. Keep these guidelines in mind: (1) Stay entirely within the gully. Do not attempt to gain the ridge to your right. Similarly, don't traverse too far to the left and leave the gully. Both of these routes are more difficult and dangerous. (2) The gully splits near the summit. Follow the right-hand fork. This will place you on the summit ridge just north of the high point. Turn right and you'll soon find a small and precarious ledge with a cairn marking the summit.

On top of Eagle, take in the full measure of Flute Glacier. From here you'll also see its massive hidden neighbor—cascading Organ Glacier—and the craggy ridge cleaving these two rivers of ice. If the weather is right you might also see the distant houses dotting Eagle River Valley, an unexpected reminder of the nearness of civilization.

18 | SYMPHONY TARNS AND TRIANGLE PEAK

Symphony Tarns
Distance: 14 miles (4 miles round trip from the hut at Eagle Lake)
Elevation Gain: 1800 feet
Hiking Time: 7 to 9 hours (2 to 3 hours from the hut at Eagle Lake)
Hike Difficulty: moderate
Terrain: rough trail, alpine tundra
High Point: 3500 feet
USGS Maps: Anchorage A-7, Anchorage B-7

Triangle Peak
Distance: 17 miles (7 miles round trip from the hut at Eagle Lake)
Elevation Gain: 3800 feet
Hiking Time: 9 to 11 hours (4 to 5 hours from the hut at Eagle Lake)
Hike Difficulty: moderate to difficult
Terrain: rough trail, alpine tundra
High Point: 5455 feet
USGS Maps: Anchorage A-7, Anchorage B-7

As overnight visitors to Eagle Lake quickly discover, flat ground on which to pitch a tent is rare. Rather than scratching out a small spot on the rocky, uneven terrain surrounding Eagle Lake, consider setting up camp at the nearby Symphony Tarns. These two placid lakes have all that you could ask for in a campsite. Situated below vertiginous mountain walls, and separated by a steep but walkable ridge, the Symphony Tarns offer seclusion, solitude, and excellent views over Eagle and Symphony Lakes. They also make a worthy day trip or staging site for a climb up Triangle Peak.

Getting There: South Fork Eagle River Valley Trailhead. From Anchorage, head north on the Glenn Highway for 10 miles and take the Eagle River Loop/Hiland Drive exit. Turn right off the exit ramp, and then right again at the first stoplight onto Hiland Drive. Follow Hiland for several miles, cross a culvert over South Fork Eagle River, and turn right onto South Creek Road. Follow this for a short distance and then make a sharp right onto West River Drive. The trailhead and a dirt parking lot are on the left, just past the turn.

Follow the Eagle Lake Trail for 5 miles to Eagle Lake. From the octagon-shaped hut near the lake, continue southeast along the ridge dividing Eagle and Symphony Lakes. Near the end of this ridge, turn right onto a small forking trail and descend a short distance toward Symphony Lake. This section of trail is overgrown with knee-high brush and can be difficult to follow.

Continue south, past the far end of Symphony Lake, and walk down to the stream feeding the lake. The valley floor is usually wet and marshy, making for unpleasant hiking. Don't travel too far up this valley—instead,

A calm day at Lower Symphony Tarn

when you're a little less than ½ mile upstream of Symphony Lake, ford the stream (best to bring a pair of sandals for this) and start hiking up the western valley wall. Climb a lichen-speckled talus slope, angling for a flat area above the stream gully on your left. Once at the top of this gully, follow the stream for ¼ mile to the first of the tarns. A small ridge divides the two tarns; climb over its base to reach the higher one.

Silently reflecting rocky cliffs and changing skies, the Symphony Tarns instill a sense of calm. They make ideal campsites with a view of the fascinating contrast in colors between Eagle and Symphony Lakes.

A short distance above the tarns lies Triangle Peak, the most easily climbed of the "Symphonic Peaks." To reach it, walk directly up the ridge between the Symphony Tarns. The ridge ends at Point 4710, the last high point before Triangle; leave the ridge about 400 feet below this point and angle left toward Triangle Pass, at the wide crest of Triangle Peak's western ridge. Turn left and follow the ridge as it curls up Triangle Peak. It drops off sharply on both sides, but is wide and safe and rises at a near-constant grade. The final push crosses some medium-sized boulders, where you'll find poor footing.

Triangle Peak divides the mostly wild from the truly wild. To the north lies South Fork Valley, at times busy with hikers; to the south is remote Ewe Valley, crowded instead with Dall sheep. Triangle's eastern ridge leads to Calliope, Flute, and Organ Peaks, several of the more forbidding mountains in the park. In contrast, Triangle and the tarns below are quiet, calm, and inviting.

19 | EWE VALLEY BACKCOUNTRY

Distance: 16 miles or more (see below)
Elevation Gain: 2300 feet
Hiking Time: 2 days or longer
Hike Difficulty: moderate to difficult
Terrain: alpine tundra, scree
High Point: 4300 feet
USGS Maps: Anchorage A-7, Anchorage B-7

For every valley in Chugach State Park with a hiking trail, many others remain untracked. Ewe Valley is one such area, included in this guide as a place to explore. There is no specific trail information or map here because there's no trail to follow. In fact, this valley has no official name; we call it Ewe Valley after the massive, craggy peak towering at its eastern edge, and for the herds of Dall sheep that call it home. It's stunning to see so many of

Descending into the Ewe Valley backcountry

these elegant, agile creatures confidently scrambling across endless slopes of black scree.

Getting There: South Fork Eagle River Valley Trailhead. From Anchorage, head north on the Glenn Highway for 10 miles and take the Eagle River Loop/Hiland Drive exit. Turn right off the exit ramp, and then right again at the first stoplight onto Hiland Drive. Follow Hiland for several miles, cross a bridge over South Fork Eagle River, and turn right onto South

Creek Road. Follow this for a short distance and then make a sharp right onto West River Drive. The trailhead and a dirt parking lot are on the left, just past the turn.

Getting to Ewe Valley from the trailhead takes a bit of effort. Follow the Eagle Lake Trail for 5 miles to Eagle Lake, then climb past Symphony Lake and the Symphony Tarns to Triangle Pass as described in Hike 18. Ewe Valley lies just over the pass. Descend south from the pass down a steep gully. Once on the valley floor, turn left (east) to continue up the valley, which ends after 3 miles in a large cirque below Mount Ewe. The open tundra makes for excellent walking, and water is readily available.

Swift hikers can depart from South Fork Trailhead in the morning, cross Triangle Pass by the late afternoon, camp in Ewe Valley, and hike out the following day. For a somewhat more relaxed pace, camp the first night at Triangle Pass (water is usually available from snow patches) or the Symphony Tarns. Then make a day trip to Ewe Valley with a light pack, stashing your tent and sleeping bag at the pass. (Be sure to include the Ten Essentials in your pack.)

A walk in Ewe Valley can range from a short ramble around the valley floor to an arduous ascent of Ewe Pass and Point 5505 atop the south valley wall. There's no definitive destination, only wilderness to explore.

Chugach State Park is full of places like Ewe Valley. Spend a few minutes poring over a topographical map and devise a route to any number of isolated passes, peaks, and valleys. Whether you head to Ewe Valley or develop your own backcountry outing, be sure to pack all the essentials—you will need to be self-reliant in this remote country. But with this responsibility comes the freedom to explore, alone with the sheep, the mountains, and the sky.

20 | RENDEZVOUS PEAK

Distance: 4 miles
Elevation Gain: 1500 feet
Hiking Time: 2½ to 4 hours
Hike Difficulty: easy
Terrain: established trail
High Point: 4000 feet
USGS Maps: Anchorage A-7, Anchorage B-7

With a clear trail across open tundra, solid footing, and a route that never climbs too steeply, Rendezvous is a great climb for kids and beginning hikers. Nearby ski lifts and an abandoned military installation compromise the area's wildness, but add a certain intrigue to the hike. Come in late

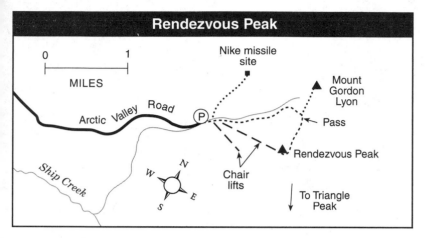

summer and you will find the hillsides draped in wildflowers and a variety of berries ripe for the picking.

Getting There: Rendezvous Peak Trailhead. From Anchorage, drive north on the Glenn Highway to the Arctic Valley exit, 2 miles beyond Muldoon Road. Follow Arctic Valley Road beyond a golf course and up several steep, wide switchbacks. After 7 dusty miles you'll reach Alpenglow Ski Area. Turn left at a fork in the road and park in a large lot near Alpenglow Ski Lodge. The Anchorage Ski Club operates the parking area and charges a parking fee. Note that Alaska State Parks parking passes are not valid at this trailhead.

From the parking lot, look uphill to where the main ski lift ends; Rendezvous Peak sits at the left end of this ridge. The trail climbs along a streambed to a pass just north of Rendezvous, then turns right and heads up to the summit. Berry pickers have worn a number of smaller trails into the ski slopes and on nearby hills. This is a popular late-summer activity: come in August and you are certain to see platoons of pickers, buckets in hand, searching for blueberries, mossberries, crowberries, and cranberries.

Walk north from the ski lodge, beneath the T-bar and chairlift. From here, a dirt trail leads northeast, up a prominent stream valley. Follow this trail, keeping the ski slopes on your right. Ignore a side trail ¼ mile up the main trail, which leads uphill underneath the chairlift. Keep instead to the main path, which follows the stream all the way to the 3468-foot pass. Depending on the time of year, the trail can be muddy in places.

It is 1 mile from the parking lot to the pass, where the park's northern peaks come brilliantly into view. Rendezvous Peak is 600 vertical feet above the pass, a short hop up the ridge to your right. Mount Gordon Lyon, the peak opposite the pass from Rendezvous, is also easily climbed from the pass (just turn left and head uphill) and is worth visiting.

Heavy use is beginning to erode the final hill leading from the pass up

to Rendezvous Peak. Stick to the main trail, which wraps around the peak, rather than following the ridge directly. After traversing for ½ mile along the ridgeline, the main trail turns sharply right. This last segment is steeper, but still manageable, even for young children.

Several prominent white buildings dot the ridge opposite Rendezvous Peak. These constitute a now-abandoned Nike missile site, built by the U.S. Army during the height of the Cold War to defend Alaska against Soviet missile attacks. For years, armed troops guarded the nuclear arsenal, warning off curious berry-pickers. Time passed too quickly for the site, though, and by the late 1970s the military closed it down and decommissioned the weapons.

If you'd rather escape the scars left by military developments and ski lifts, hike along the ridge stretching southeast from Rendezvous Peak. You can follow its dips and rises for nearly 10 miles to Triangle Peak (the destination of Hike 18). Return along the ridge to Rendezvous Peak Trailhead, or drop down from Triangle Pass to the spectacular Symphony Tarns and into South Fork Eagle River Valley, where you can pick up the Eagle Lake Trail and return to civilization.

Lowbush blueberries, a tasty mountain treat
(Photo courtesy of Chugach State Park)

THE WEST PARK

The western region of Chugach State Park is Anchorage's true backyard. Many trails begin right in town, and its peaks dominate the city's eastern skyline. Bounded by the city to the west and Ship Creek to the north and east, it has a character distinct from the rest of the park. It's a little less rugged and wild. Most of its hikes follow well-maintained trails, including the park's most popular walk, Flattop Mountain. There are no glaciers, although you'll see abundant evidence of past glaciation.

Here you'll find some of the park's most memorable spots, such as shimmering Black Lake beneath the sheer north face of O'Malley Peak, and the narrow, pinnacled summit of The Ramp. And certainly the western park *does* have its remote corners. Visit the windswept heights of the Tanaina Peaks, or crash through mud bogs and brush along the Ship Creek Valley Trail. You're likely to be alone with the wilderness on either of these hikes.

The peaks west of Ship Creek form a dramatic backdrop for Anchorage, a constant reminder of the nearby wilderness. They're justifiably popular hiking destinations, and many enthusiastic hikers make a point of climbing all the major peaks on the skyline. Ten rise higher than 5000 feet: Temptation Peak, Tikishla Peak, East Tanaina Peak, Koktoya Peak, The Ramp, Avalanche Peak, O'Malley Peak, Mount Williwaw, and the North and South Suicide Peaks. Some of these mountains have rough trails leading to their summits, while others require some moderate scrambling. All are exciting climbs with challenging routes and impressive views.

The peaks of western Chugach State Park rise above Anchorage. (Photo courtesy of Chugach State Park)

21 | SNOW HAWK VALLEY AND TEMPTATION PEAK

Upper Snow Hawk Cabin
Distance: 12 miles
Elevation Gain: 2300 feet
Hiking Time: 5 to 7 hours
Hike Difficulty: moderate
Terrain: established trail, rough trail
High Point: 2650 feet
USGS Maps: Anchorage A-7, Anchorage A-8

Temptation Peak
Distance: 17 miles
Elevation Gain: 5100 feet
Hiking Time: 10 to 14 hours (or overnight)
Hike Difficulty: moderate to difficult
Terrain: alpine tundra, scree
High Point: 5350 feet
USGS Maps: Anchorage A-7, Anchorage A-8

Though surrounded on three sides by Chugach State Park, Snow Hawk Valley actually belongs to the United States Army. It's a wilderness area, with an excellent hiking trail leading through the underbrush and into the upper valley. Call the military police at (907) 384-0823 to confirm access and make sure no military maneuvers are being performed in the area. Be respectful of any U.S. military personnel you may encounter and be aware that you are hiking at your own risk. The Army built two small cabins in the Valley; the lower one, tucked among birches, has unfortunately burned down. A second cabin, sits high on the open valley floor. There's a lot to see in this expansive valley, but the best destinations are the upper Snow Hawk Cabin (a squat little shelter seemingly dropped at random in the middle of the tundra) and Temptation Peak with its stunning tarn.

Getting There: Snow Hawk Valley Trailhead. Drive north from Anchorage on the Glenn Highway and exit on Arctic Valley Road, 2 miles past Muldoon Road. Continue on Arctic Valley past a golf course. About ½ mile farther, bear right on a dirt road marked with signs reading "Snow Hawk Cabins." This road soon dead-ends at a yellow gate. Park here and continue past the gate on foot.

Once past the parking area, follow a dirt road over a bridge and to an immediate intersection. Bear left and continue for about ⅓ mile. At a wide curve in the road, follow signs for the military rappelling grounds.

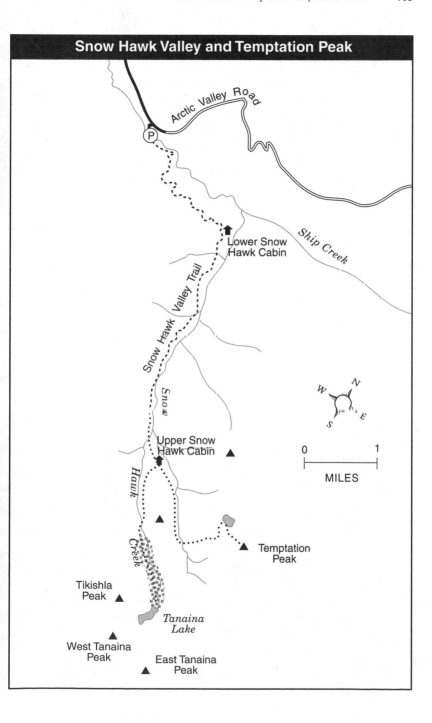

Snow Hawk Valley and Temptation Peak

Arctic Valley Road

P

Lower Snow Hawk Cabin

Ship Creek

Snow Hawk Valley Trail

Snow

Upper Snow Hawk Cabin

▲

N
W   E
S

0   1

MILES

▲

Temptation Peak

▲

Hawk

Creek

Tikishla Peak ▲

Tanaina Lake

West Tanaina Peak ▲

East Tanaina Peak ▲

These lead to a trail that initially parallels a chain link fence. After a short distance, you'll come to a split in the trail. Take the right branch, marked "Snow Hawk Cabins."

The first several miles of the trail are overgrown. As you slowly rise through the forest, keep an eye out for strips of red tape tied to branches and small metallic signs—marked "trail"—nailed to tree trunks at eye level. After 2 miles of steady climbing, you'll see the charred remains of the lower Snow Hawk Cabin slightly to the left of the trail.

The trail continues for another 1½ miles beyond the remains of the cabin (watch for the trail markers) and then climbs onto open tundra in the upper Snow Hawk Valley. The upper Snow Hawk Cabin sits at the base of a large ridge cleaving the upper valley in two. The trail peters out shortly before the cabin, which can be surprisingly difficult to find in the rolling terrain; take a mental note of its location from a distance to avoid aimless searching. The cozy little structure makes a good turn-around point, and also offers a place to dry out and eat lunch before exploring the valley. Hikers with military affiliation can reserve the cabin by calling the Outdoor Recreation Center on Fort Richardson at (907) 384-1476.

A worthy destination in the upper valley is Tanaina Lake, a large tarn

Temptation Peak rises above a stunning tarn.

located 2½ miles up the right-hand fork of the upper Snow Hawk Valley. As you stand on the tarn's shores, ringed by ramparts of sharp, crumbling peaks, with only the sound of wind blowing across the tundra, you'll find it hard to believe that a sprawling city lies just behind the valley walls.

A more strenuous but rewarding objective is Temptation Peak, one of the park's grandest mountains. Cut off from the other peaks near Anchorage, Temptation remained unclimbed until famed mountaineer Vin Hoeman painstakingly bushwhacked his way up its eastern slopes in 1963. Luckily, there is now an easier route, but it's still a long trip from Snow Hawk Trailhead to Temptation's summit and back. Start early or plan on camping in the upper valley.

To reach Temptation Peak, continue east from the upper Snow Hawk Cabin, heading up the left-hand (eastern) fork of the upper Snow Hawk Valley. Follow the valley floor for about 1 mile. From here, climb northeast up a shallow gully on your left. Near the top, the gully widens. Bear west slightly, aiming for a flat area above you. From the crest of this rise, a brilliant sight unfolds: hidden in Temptation's shadow lies a sunken tarn, deep aqua green against the blue sky, enclosed by near-vertical walls of rock.

From the tarn, head east around its south side and begin climbing a ridge that leads directly to Temptation's summit. Be wary of the steep cliffs dropping to your left; stick instead to the gentle talus slopes on the right. Once at the narrow summit, sign the register and marvel at the expansive valleys and peaks below. Descend as you came, or explore the ridge extending south toward the Tanaina Peaks. Avoid Temptation's craggy north ridge, where steep gullies and loose rock make for a dangerous descent.

22 | SHIP CREEK VALLEY TRAIL

Distance: 20 miles (one-way traverse)
Elevation Gain: 1300 feet (from north to south)
Hiking Time: 1 to 3 days
Hike Difficulty: difficult
Terrain: rough trail, backcountry
High Point: 2350 feet
USGS Maps: Anchorage A-7, Seward D-7

The wide and wild Ship Creek Valley arcs gracefully into the mountains behind Anchorage, dividing the park's familiar and well-traveled foothills from its more remote regions. Though it straddles this border, the Ship Creek Valley Trail is definitely not a well-worn path. Thick, dark stands of birch and spruce drop a perpetually moist twilight over the riverbank; higher in the valley, swaths of fireweed, cow parsnip, and alder crowd your

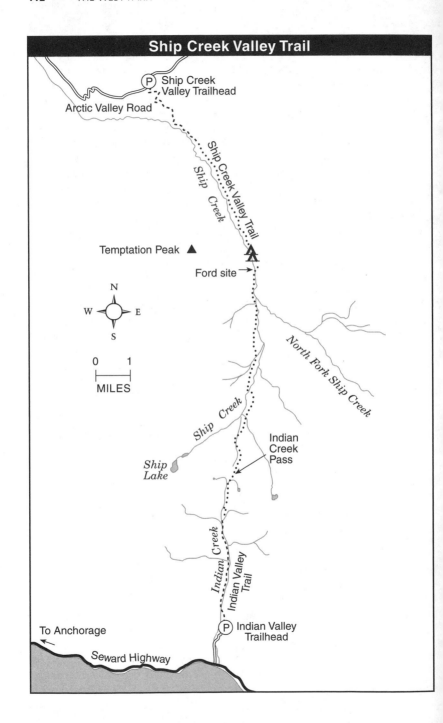

Ship Creek Valley Trail

P Ship Creek Valley Trailhead

Arctic Valley Road

Ship Creek Valley Trail

Ship Creek

Temptation Peak ▲

Ford site

N
W E
S

0   1
MILES

North Fork Ship Creek

Ship Creek

Ship Lake

Indian Creek Pass

Indian Creek

Indian Valley Trail

To Anchorage

P Indian Valley Trailhead

Seward Highway

feet and legs. At Indian Creek Pass, the sparser valley floor is pocked with curious dips and rises, hinting at the giant moraine buried beneath fragile tundra. Hiking in this rugged land requires fortitude, but for a compact journey through the heart of the wilderness, over a mile-wide pass ringed with jagged peaks, and down to the pale gray ocean, this trip can't be beat.

Ship Creek Valley remains, true to the intentions of the park's founders, a pristine wilderness—so don't expect any mileposts or trail maintenance. In fact, don't expect a trail. There *is* a patchy path of sorts, rarely obvious and always rough, but a dogged determination to follow it through the thick and thicker will lead only to frustration. Treat this hike as a backcountry trek: use the trail where you find it, and pick your way through brush, forests, and tundra where you do not. On even the sunniest of days, bring rain pants and extra socks; the undergrowth, mud, and river crossing make these a necessity.

Getting There: Ship Creek Valley and Indian Valley Trailheads. This hike starts at Ship Creek Valley Trailhead and finishes at Indian Valley Trailhead. Park a car at each end or arrange for a pick up. To reach Ship Creek Valley Trailhead, drive north from Anchorage on the Glenn Highway and take the Arctic Valley exit, 2 miles beyond Muldoon Road. Follow Arctic Valley Road beyond a golf course (where it soon turns to gravel) and up several steep, wide switchbacks. After 6½ miles, park at a turnout on your right, across the road from a gate. Look for a small sign marking the trailhead.

To reach Indian Valley Trailhead, drive south on the Seward Highway from downtown Anchorage. At mile 103.1, just past the Indian Road intersection, turn left onto a dirt road named Ocean View Drive, immediately before the Turnagain House Restaurant. Slow down and look carefully; this turn is easy to miss. The road skirts the restaurant parking lot and continues into the woods. After ½ mile, bear right at an intersection marked by a Chugach State Park sign. This road ends ¾ mile later at the trailhead.

From the Ship Creek parking area, the trail descends 900 feet to the valley floor, and reaches a major intersection after about ½ mile. Go left (east) and continue through encroaching brush. Ignore side forks as you head south and east. The first part of the hike is on U.S. Army land, but roughly 2 miles from the trailhead you'll cross the Chugach State Park boundary. Expect diminishing trail quality beyond this point.

The trail soon reaches the valley floor and then parallels Ship Creek for 6 miles, meandering through serene mixed forests. At times the walking is easy and a trail is obvious. At other times the trail suddenly disappears, leaving no clear indication of the way forward. Map and compass skills are essential, but by staying relatively near the river you should not get too far off course. Approximately 7 miles from the trailhead, close to the river, are several potential campsites—a good first night's stop for a 3-day trip.

Shortly after the campsites, the "trail" crosses Ship Creek. Orange stakes mark both sides of an established ford site. This is not the only suitable crossing, though, so don't despair if you can't find the stakes. Just

Subalpine tundra near Indian Creek Pass

remember that you *must* cross Ship Creek at some point soon, lest you mistakenly branch into North Fork Ship Creek Valley (a vast, wonderful place, but far afield from your destination). Start looking for the ford site when the craggy pinnacles of Temptation Peak are directly to the west.

Across the river, the hiking becomes more challenging. This part of the trail is *never* maintained; expect to negotiate chest-high grasses, uneven ground, and several bogs. Hike parallel to the river (now on the west bank) for the next several miles. Try climbing a hundred feet or so above the river for drier ground. You might spot metallic yellow triangles nailed to trees at eye level indicating the path of least resistance. These signs guide skiers in the winter, but are of only marginal use to summer hikers.

As you head farther south, the valley narrows, the ground gets drier, and the alder thickens. Approximately 3 miles after the ford site, an honest-to-goodness trail re-emerges, marked periodically by orange stakes. The next few miles cross wide-open high country. About 4 miles beyond the ford site, the trail (still at times hard to follow) crosses back to the eastern side of the Ship Creek headwaters. This second ford site is not well-marked—just find a place where you can get through the brush. About 1½ miles later, the trail crosses the creek yet again and climbs toward Indian Creek Pass, a nebulous high point in a broad, flat expanse. However, the Indian Valley Trail (which begins at the pass) is unmistakable, thanks to bona fide trail maintenance. (See Hike 41 for a full description of the Indian Valley Trail.) From the pass, follow the trail along Indian Creek for 5 miles through high meadows and lush boreal forests to Indian Valley Trailhead.

23 | THE DOME AND LONG LAKE

The Dome
Distance: 5½ miles
Elevation Gain: 1900 feet
Hiking Time: 3 to 4 hours
Hike Difficulty: easy
Terrain: established trail
High Point: 2800 feet
USGS Map: Anchorage A-8

Long Lake
Distance: 15½ miles
Elevation Gain: 2800 feet
Hiking Time: 7 to 10 hours
Hike Difficulty: moderate
Terrain: rough trail, alpine tundra
High Point: 3100 feet
USGS Maps: Anchorage A-7, Anchorage A-8

This hike follows a narrow trail from Stuckagain Heights to a rounded high point unofficially dubbed "The Dome." Gentle slopes dotted with blueberry bushes and fireweed, close views of Anchorage, and easy access to North Fork Campbell Creek Valley are among the high points of this hike. Although The Dome lies just beyond the state park boundaries, you'll rarely have any company other than a few fellow hikers, runners, and the occasional horseback rider.

Beyond The Dome, in the North Fork Campbell Creek Valley, sits pristine Long Lake, ringed by crumbling peaks. For being so near Anchorage, this lake rarely draws crowds. Getting there involves an ambitious day trip; it's a good idea to camp near the lake and spend an extra day either exploring the nearby mountains or making a loop around the Williwaw Lakes to Glen Alps Trailhead (Hike 33).

Getting There: Stuckagain Heights Trailhead. The Dome trail begins near the top of Stuckagain Heights Road in East Anchorage. From downtown Anchorage, drive south through town on the Seward Highway to the Tudor Road exit. Turn left and head east, toward the mountains. (The Dome will be directly ahead on the horizon, a rounded hill scarred by a wide dirt trail.) After driving for 3¼ miles down Tudor Road, turn right onto Campbell Airstrip Road. This becomes Basher Drive. Follow Basher for 4½ miles, ignoring side roads. Park in a wide clearing where the road ends, just before it heads up a steep hill to end at some new home sites.

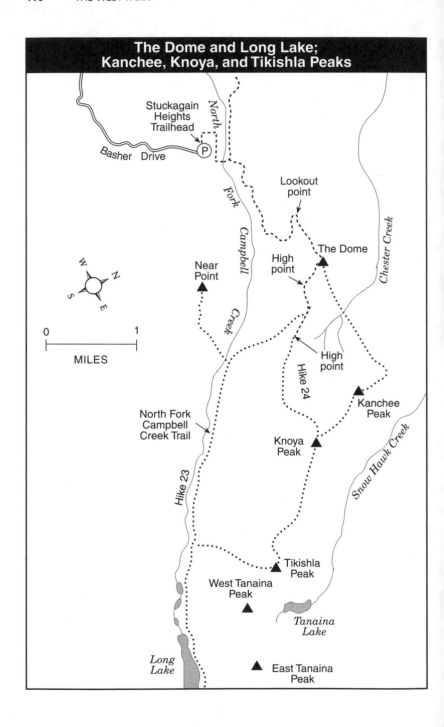

The Dome and Long Lake; Kanchee, Knoya, and Tikishla Peaks

Stream crossing on the Dome Trail (Photo by Morrie Shepherd)

On foot, follow a road heading downhill beneath powerlines for about ¼ mile, where it levels off. Here turn right onto a side trail, slightly overgrown, that switches back and leads down to North Fork Campbell Creek. Once at the creek, follow the trail upstream for a short distance to a small bridge reaching across the swift creek. On the far side, the trail climbs several switchbacks to a T intersection. Bear right. Make a mental note of this unmarked intersection, as it's easy to miss on the way down.

From this intersection it's 2 more miles to The Dome. The trail is generally good but can be overgrown and eroded in places. There is an excellent lookout from atop a small knob just before the final, ¾-mile long rise to the summit. If you've come for a bird's-eye view of the city, stop here—you will not find a more expansive one anywhere in the park. Otherwise, climb steadily eastward to The Dome's rounded summit.

To reach North Fork Campbell Creek Valley, continue over the top of The Dome and follow a small trail southeast. Climb a second small rise and then drop to a saddle. Continue east along the ridge to reach Knoya (see Hike 24); otherwise, drop from the ridge and traverse southeast across the hillside, maintaining a consistent elevation. After traversing for about ½ mile you'll be past most of the brush that clogs the lower valley. Drop to the main valley floor, where the walking is delightful. It's an easy 3 miles farther to Long Lake.

(A similar but slightly longer approach to North Fork Valley can be made by starting from Prospect Heights Trailhead and hiking up Near Point (Hike 26). Descend Near Point's southeast ridge to a wide saddle. From here, drop northeast to the North Fork Valley floor.)

Long Lake makes a memorable campsite, but remember to pitch your tent at least a hundred yards from the water. The Tanaina Peaks and Koktoya Peak (Hike 25) offer challenging side trips. For a less strenuous continuation, make your way past Long Lake and through the narrow corridor between Mount Williwaw and Mount Elliot into Middle Fork Campbell Creek Valley. From here you can hike out to either Glen Alps or Prospect Heights along the Williwaw Lakes Trail (Hike 33). For an excellent 3-day trip, hike in and camp at Long Lake; on the second day, climb one of the nearby peaks and move camp to the Williwaw Lakes; and enjoy a relaxed hike out to Glen Alps or Prospect Heights on the third day.

24 | KANCHEE, KNOYA, AND TIKISHLA PEAKS

Kanchee and Knoya Loop
Distance: 10½ miles
Elevation Gain: 4400 feet
Hiking Time: 6 to 8 hours
Hike Difficulty: moderate
Terrain: rough trail, alpine tundra
High Point: 4600 feet
USGS Maps: Anchorage A-7, Anchorage A-8

Tikishla
Distance: 13½ miles
Elevation Gain: 5000 feet
Hiking Time: 8 to 10 hours
Hike Difficulty: moderate to difficult
Terrain: rough trail, scrambling
High Point: 5150 feet
USGS Maps: Anchorage A-7, Anchorage A-8

While hikers frequently climb the mountains bordering North Fork Campbell Creek on its south side (Near Point and Wolverine), the peaks bordering this valley to the north are often ignored. Kanchee Peak, Knoya Peak, and Tikishla Peak—ascending in both height and order of difficulty—

Tikishla Peak in early spring

all make for excellent hikes, either from Stuckagain Heights Trailhead or from a campsite in Campbell Creek or Chester Creek Valleys. The mountains take their names from the Dena'ina language: Kanchee means "porcupine," Knoya "beaver," and Tikishla "black bear." You won't see any of these lowland animals on the peaks themselves, but keep an eye out for Dall sheep, marmots, and bald eagles.

Getting There: Stuckagain Heights Trailhead. From downtown Anchorage, drive south through town on the Seward Highway to the Tudor Road exit. Turn left and head east, toward the mountains. After driving for 3¼ miles down Tudor Road, turn right onto Campbell Airstrip Road. This becomes Basher Drive when the pavement ends. Follow Basher for 4½ miles, ignoring side roads. Park in a wide clearing where the road ends, just outside the Near Point Knoll subdivision.

From the trailhead, follow a dirt road downhill beneath powerlines for about ¼ mile. Turn right on a side trail and follow it through switchbacks to North Fork Campbell Creek, then upstream a short distance to a bridge. Cross the creek and follow the trail to the rounded summit of The Dome (Hike 23). Kanchee Peak rises directly east from The Dome. Knoya Peak, even higher, lies ½ mile along Kanchee's southern ridge.

To surmount Knoya and Kanchee with minimal elevation gain, head south on a sheep trail from The Dome to a nearby high point. Continue along this ridge, walking high above the North Fork Campbell Creek Valley floor, for ½ mile until you reach another high point. From here the ridge makes a wide bend and rises steadily over the next 2 miles to a false summit of Knoya. Head over the false summit and along even terrain to reach the true peak.

The ridge heading north to Kanchee is equally inviting, and returning to The Dome via Kanchee is no harder than retracing your steps along the first ridge. From Knoya, backtrack to the false summit and descend north to the saddle between Knoya and Kanchee. You can skirt around several bumps on the ridge by traversing across the western side of the ridge, but beware of the eastern side, which drops steeply into Snow Hawk Valley. (Look carefully and you'll see the upper Snow Hawk Cabin gleaming on the valley floor.) The ridge is easily walkable the entire way to Kanchee.

To climb only Kanchee, you can head straight east from The Dome, descending into Chester Creek Valley, and head up the mountain's eastern face. Make your way along a low ridge rising to a notch between Kanchee and a small bump on its northern ridge. The path to this notch is less steep than other routes up the mountain. Turn right at the notch and head to Kanchee's summit, ¼ mile away. Return as you came.

If Tikishla is your goal, be prepared for a grueling but rewarding route. From the summit of Knoya, continue southeast along a slowly descending ridge. The walking is easy and fairly level. After 1 mile you'll reach the base of Tikishla's fierce western face, where the ridge swings sharply upward. Follow the ridge as closely as possible, using your hands for balance and traversing to your right as necessary. After climbing 700 feet, you'll reach a false summit; head directly east for ¼ mile to the true summit, which hangs precipitously between Long Lake to the south and Tanaina Lake to the east. Competent scramblers can continue along the ridge to East and West Tanaina and Koktoya Peaks (Hike 25), or "ski" down the scree slope on Tikishla's southern face and trek upvalley to Long Lake. Otherwise, return along the ridge to Knoya and The Dome.

25 | TANAINA PEAKS AND KOKTOYA PEAK

Distance: 17 to 19 miles (from Stuckagain Heights Trailhead)
Elevation Gain: 5300 feet or 5100 feet
Hiking Time: 10 to 14 hours
Hike Difficulty: moderate to difficult
Terrain: scree, scrambling
High Point: 5350 feet or 5100 feet
USGS Maps: Anchorage A-6, Anchorage A-7

Many devoted Chugach climbers, at one time or another, aim to climb all ten peaks west of Ship Creek that rise higher than 5000 feet. This isn't an easy job—some of these summits require routefinding and moderate scrambling. Some are less difficult to surmount, but lie high above and far from any trailhead. Such is the case with East Tanaina and Koktoya Peaks, two remote mountains crowding the shores of Long Lake. They both

A hiker explores the wilderness around Long Lake.

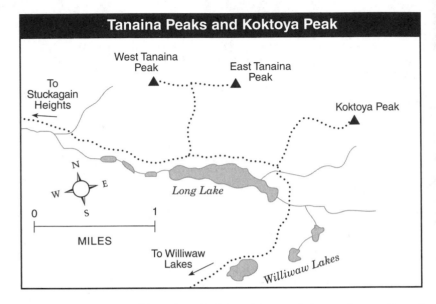

Tanaina Peaks and Koktoya Peak

West Tanaina Peak

East Tanaina Peak

To Stuckagain Heights

Koktoya Peak

N

W E

S

Long Lake

0 1

MILES

To Williwaw Lakes

Williwaw Lakes

demand a little scrambling, but climbing either peak is mostly a matter of perseverance. It's a long trek to either summit from the trailhead, so plan on starting very early or making camp at the lake.

Getting There: Stuckagain Heights Trailhead. From downtown Anchorage, drive south through town on the Seward Highway to the Tudor Road exit. Turn left and head east, toward the mountains. After driving for 3¼ miles down Tudor Road, turn right onto Campbell Airstrip Road. This becomes Basher Drive when the pavement ends. Follow Basher for 5 miles, ignoring side roads. Park in a wide clearing on the left side of the road, just before it heads up a steep hill to housing sites.

Begin at Stuckagain Heights Trailhead and follow the trail over The Dome into North Fork Campbell Creek Valley (Hike 23). Continue upvalley to Long Lake. Four of the ten 5000-foot summits in this part of the park—Tikishla Peak, East Tanaina Peak, Koktoya Peak, and Mount Williwaw—lie within a mile of the lake, making it an ideal base camp for mountain walking. While Tikishla (Hike 24) is usually approached from the lower North Fork Valley, and Williwaw (Hike 35) from the Williwaw Lakes Trail, East Tanaina Peak and Koktoya are best climbed directly from the lake.

There is no trail up either mountain—both involve a moderate scramble up scree slopes, followed by a ridge walk to the summit. For East Tanaina Peak, start at the western end of Long Lake and climb directly north up a broad, shallow gully. After gaining 1700 feet of elevation, you'll reach a prominent saddle between East and West Tanaina Peaks. You can reach either summit from this saddle; East Tanaina, ½ mile to the right, is the higher one. Scramble along the ridge crest, watching out for loose rock.

Like many peaks in this area, East Tanaina's mellow southern face contrasts sharply with the vertiginous north face, which drops more than 1500 feet to remote Tanaina Lake. A ridge runs north from East Tanaina around this lake, extending 3 miles to Temptation Peak. Experienced scramblers can traverse the entire distance, though the route is difficult and exposed in several areas. When returning to Long Lake from either Tanaina summit, descend as you came, via the saddle.

Koktoya Peak lies just east of the Tanaina Peaks. Hike to the eastern end of Long Lake, then scramble northeast up to a narrow, steep-walled saddle between East Tanaina and Koktoya Peaks. At this pass, leave the ridge and strike out across Koktoya's southwest face. Traverse eastward and slightly uphill for about ¼ mile, and then turn uphill and either climb back to Koktoya's western ridge or head straight for the summit. On top, a small patch of flat earth invites you to rest and admire the view. Tufts of grass make an unexpected and welcome contrast to the endless fields of gray scree below. Descend as you came, or climb down the south ridge to a saddle below Mount Williwaw and descend west along a buttressing ridge to Long Lake.

26 | NEAR POINT AND WOLVERINE PEAK

Near Point
Distance: 7 miles
Elevation Gain: 2000 feet
Hiking Time: 4 to 6 hours
Hike Difficulty: easy
Terrain: established trail, alpine tundra
High Point: 3050 feet
USGS Map: Anchorage A-8

Wolverine Peak
Distance: 10 miles
Elevation Gain: 3400 feet
Hiking Time: 6 to 8 hours
Hike Difficulty: moderate
Terrain: established trail
High Point: 4455 feet
USGS Maps: Anchorage A-7, Anchorage A-8

Locals and outsiders alike sometimes remark of Anchorage that it is "only twenty minutes from Alaska." Some intend this as an insult to Alaska's metropolis, while others say it with pride. In either case, mountains like

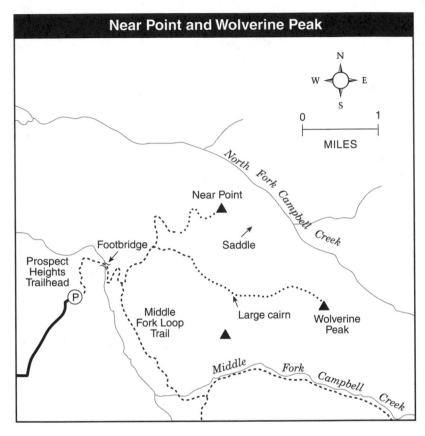

Near Point and Wolverine Peak

Near Point and Wolverine Peak illustrate the point. Sitting right in Anchorage's backyard, they prove that one need not stray far from downtown to find true wilderness.

Both mountains, reached from Prospect Heights Trailhead, make fine day outings. Near Point, its lower slopes dotted with houses, is a good first peak for young hikers. Wolverine, much higher, rises gently from a large valley and forms a natural amphitheater of sorts. People climb it year-round, in summer sun and winter twilight. The mountain is arguably at its best in autumn, when blazing fireweed and ripe berries paint the slopes in a riot of color. Termination dust (an Alaskan term for winter's first snowfall, at which time the brief, manic construction season terminates) arrives soon thereafter, bringing a different mood to the mountain.

Getting There: Prospect Heights Trailhead. From downtown Anchorage, drive 7 miles south on the Seward Highway and take the O'Malley Road exit. Turn left (east) on O'Malley and follow it toward the mountains for 3¾ miles, where it bears left and becomes Hillside Drive. After bearing left, take an immediate right turn onto Upper O'Malley Drive. Follow Upper O'Malley for ½ mile to an intersection and then turn left onto Prospect Drive. Follow this for 1 mile to Prospect Heights Trailhead. You'll find ample parking and toilets; expect a day-use fee.

From the trailhead notice board, follow a wide track east for several hundred feet into the woods, then bear left at the first intersection. Continue on this trail over a small rise and down to South Fork Campbell Creek, about 1 mile from the trailhead. Cross a footbridge and climb through switchbacks to a second intersection and veer left (the right-hand trail is the Middle Fork Loop, Hike 27). Approximately 1 mile after the footbridge, you'll reach the Near Point/Wolverine intersection.

For Near Point, proceed north (straight ahead at the intersection) on the well-worn trail. You'll soon leave the trees behind. Ground squirrels are abundant, as are blueberries in the fall. The final push to the summit crosses bare, rocky tundra; the trail fades but the route is obvious. The summit, rising just above hillside homes, feels more part of the city than the state park. Retrace your steps to return to the trailhead, or turn southeast and continue along the ridge for a more ambitious traverse to Wolverine. The saddle between Near Point and Wolverine also offers good access to Long Lake (Hike 23).

To visit Wolverine Peak, bear right at the Near Point/Wolverine intersection and climb east through thinning brush. After another ¾ miles, the

Winter solstice on Wolverine Peak

trail emerges into a high valley and gains the crest of a prominent buttress-ing ridge. Make a sharp left turn here. A large cairn marks the spot; do not miss this turn on your way back down. The trail climbs gradually and con-sistently for another 1½ miles to the summit. If you lose the trail on the rocky upper slopes, simply follow Wolverine's northwest ridge to its apex. A wrecked and rusted airplane litters the slopes near the top, a jarring sight in this pristine landscape.

Note: As of this update in 2006, a new trail has been developed to access Near Point and neighboring trails from East Anchorage. The trailhead is 3.2 miles up Basher Drive (see Hike #23 for directions to Basher Drive; look for a small parking area on the right. The trail initially follows under powerlines and then heads east along the rim of a canyon. It joins the Near Point trail at its junction with the Wolverine Peak Trail. From here you can continue to either peak or turn south toward the Hillside trailheads (see Hikes #26 and #27).

27 | MIDDLE FORK LOOP AND HILLSIDE TRAILS

Middle Fork Loop
Distance: 9 miles (complete loop)
Elevation Gain: 1400 feet
Hiking Time: 4 to 6 hours
Hike Difficulty: easy
Terrain: established trail
High Point: 2100 feet
USGS Map: Anchorage A-8

A wealth of trails cover the western Chugach foothills, perfect for days when the time or energy for a longer hike is lacking. Lying on the outskirts of Anchorage, these trails are mostly flat and keep to forested lowlands, offering any number of quiet afternoon rambles. Though popular with lo-cals, especially for skiing and snowshoeing in the winter, the trails are hardly crowded. Start from any of the trailheads mentioned below and de-sign a loop to suit your ambition. Keep track of your way back to your trailhead, since not all trails are well-marked. There are several smaller trails in the area and still more in the Municipality of Anchorage Far North Bicentennial Park, northwest of Prospect Heights. What follows is not a complete listing, only the major trails in this extensive network.

Getting There: Anchorage Hillside Trailheads
Prospect Heights Trailhead. From downtown Anchorage, drive 7 miles

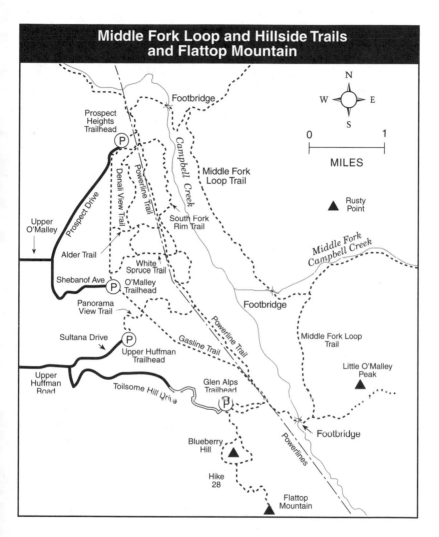

Middle Fork Loop and Hillside Trails and Flattop Mountain

south on the Seward Highway and take the O'Malley Road exit. Turn left (east) on O'Malley and follow it toward the mountains for 3¾ miles, where it bears left and becomes Hillside Drive. After bearing left, take an immediate right turn onto Upper O'Malley Drive. Follow O'Malley for ½ mile to an intersection and then turn left onto Prospect Drive. Follow this for 1 mile to Prospect Heights Trailhead.

O'Malley Trailhead. From downtown Anchorage, drive 7 miles south on the Seward Highway and take the O'Malley Road exit. Turn left onto O'Malley Road and follow it toward the mountains for 3¾ miles, where it bears left and becomes Hillside Drive. Immediately after bearing left, turn right onto Upper O'Malley Drive. Follow it ½ mile to an intersection and bear right at Trails End Road, then left onto Shebanof Avenue, which dead-ends at the small trailhead.

Upper Huffman Trailhead. Follow the above directions to O'Malley Road. From O'Malley, turn right at Hillside Drive, continue for a mile, and then turn left on Upper Huffman Road. After driving ½ mile further, bear left at the intersection onto Sultana Drive, which ends at a large parking lot.

Glen Alps Trailhead. From downtown Anchorage, drive 7 miles south on the Seward Highway and take the O'Malley Road exit. Turn left (east) onto O'Malley and follow it toward the mountains for 3½ miles. Turn right onto Hillside Drive. Follow this road for 1 mile, and then turn left onto Upper Huffman Road. Continue ¾ mile and turn right onto Toilsome Hill Drive. A Chugach State Park sign marks this intersection. Follow Toilsome Hill (which soon becomes a dirt road) up several switchbacks for about 2 miles and turn left into the trailhead parking lot.

Middle Fork Loop: This trail, the longest and most pleasant loop on the hillside, joins Glen Alps and Prospect Heights Trailheads via a high traverse across foothills. It climbs gradually from wooded Campbell Creek to the wide-open tundra and back, and encompasses much of Chugach State Park's natural diversity. It's marked and (mostly) well-maintained, save for the occasional muddy patch.

Pick up the loop at Prospect Heights Trailhead. From the trailhead notice board, follow a wide trail east for several hundred feet into the woods, to a T intersection with the Powerline Trail. Turn left and follow the trail as it climbs a small rise and then descends to South Fork Campbell Creek. Cross a footbridge and continue up switchbacks to a signposted intersection, about 2 miles from the trailhead. Take the right fork.

The trail now bends south along the lower slopes of Rusty Point. Muddy sections of the trail are covered with boardwalks. Soon you'll be out of the alders and walking on the high tundra. The trail eventually crosses Campbell Creek again on a footbridge, ascends briefly, and then forks. Signs mark the route: left for the Williwaw Lakes Trail (Hike 33) and right to continue on the Middle Fork Loop. The next 2 miles are almost always muddy throughout the spring and after rain showers. There are no boardwalks here, only meager planks strung intermittently across the mud. Previous hikers, attempting to stay dry, have created a number of detours, in effect widening the trail to a muddy highway. Stick to the main trail to help prevent further erosion.

South of Little O'Malley Peak, the Middle Fork Loop intersects The Ballpark trail. Bear right and continue downhill, across South Fork Campbell Creek on a footbridge, and up to the Powerline Trail (Hike 29) just outside Glen Alps Trailhead. Either finish your hike at Glen Alps or turn right and hike for 3 miles along the Powerline Trail to Prospect Heights.

Powerline Trail: The section of this trail running southeast from Glen Alps to Indian is described in Hike 29; the 3 miles between Glen Alps and

On the Hillside Trails

Prospect Heights are less interesting, but useful for completing a loop on one of the other trails mentioned below. The trail is an access road running underneath the powerlines and is generally well-maintained.

Gasline Trail: The Gasline Trail leaves the Powerline Trail shortly past Glen Alps and terminates at Prospect Heights. It follows over the buried gas pipes servicing Anchorage's hillside homes. It's a good trail for jogging, and also useful if you want to start a hike from O'Malley or Upper Huffman Trailheads, which are usually less crowded than Glen Alps and Prospect Heights.

White Spruce Trail, Alder Trail, and Panorama View Trail: These three shorter trails all run east to west, connecting the Gasline Trail to the Powerline Trail. Not well-maintained, they are better used in winter as ski or snowshoe trails.

Denali View Trail: This trail runs between the White Spruce and Powerline Trails. It is not well-maintained. True to its name, it offers a stunning view of Denali to the north—if the weather cooperates.

South Fork Rim Trail: This scenic, well-maintained trail makes a wide half-loop from a point near Prospect Heights to the Powerline Trail, 1 mile distant. It skirts the edge of a steep valley carved by South Fork Campbell Creek. The views are excellent.

28 | FLATTOP MOUNTAIN

Distance: 3 miles
Elevation Gain: 1300 feet
Hiking Time: 2 to 5 hours
Hike Difficulty: moderate
Terrain: established trail, scrambling
High Point: 3550 feet
USGS Map: Anchorage A-8

Flattop is climbed more often than any mountain in Alaska, and that is a mixed blessing. It boasts a high trailhead with plenty of space for parking, a short and well-maintained trail, and gorgeous summit vistas from Cook Inlet to Denali. And yet Flattop is somehow... *un-Alaskan!* Alaska is famous for its beautiful wilderness, not for its crowds. Flattop has an abundance of both, bringing to mind Yogi Berra's oft-quoted lament about a favorite restaurant: "Nobody goes there anymore, it's too crowded." On most other trails in Chugach State Park, you'll likely see a mere handful of fellow hikers; on Flattop, you might as well be strolling down Anchorage's Fourth Avenue. Still, Flattop *is* an undeniably beautiful hike and the flagship of Chugach State Park's "accessible wilderness." It's almost a tradition: sometime during the summer, enjoy a sunny evening with your friends and family atop Flattop Mountain. Just don't expect to be the only ones.

Getting There: Glen Alps Trailhead. From downtown Anchorage, drive 7 miles south on the Seward Highway and take the O'Malley Road exit. Turn left (east) onto O'Malley and follow it toward the mountains for

3½ miles. Turn right onto Hillside Drive. Follow this road for 1 mile, and then turn left onto Upper Huffman Road. Continue ¾ mile and turn right onto Toilsome Hill Drive. A Chugach State Park sign marks this intersection. Follow Toilsome Hill (which soon becomes a dirt road) up several switchbacks for about 2 miles and turn left into the trailhead parking lot. Situated at tree line, Glen Alps has ample parking, a viewing deck, and toilets. There is a day-use fee. Don't try to shirk the fee by parking outside the trailhead gate on Toilsome Hill Drive—you're almost certain to get a ticket.

Begin your hike on the prominent staircase at the parking lot's eastern end. A winding gravel path takes you through waist-high hemlocks, stunted and sharply bent by strong winds. After ¼ mile you'll reach the base of Blueberry Hill, marked by a park bench and an informative display. Turn right and follow the path around Blueberry Hill. Even at this lower elevation the view is impressive. Less ambitious hikers may be content to complete the Blueberry Hill Loop (2 miles total) and return to the parking lot.

If you have your eyes on the peak, turn right at the well-marked intersection on the far side of Blueberry Hill. A large-scale volunteer effort spanning several summers recently developed this new trail up Flattop. It slowly traverses the mountain's west flank, providing views of South Anchorage and Rabbit Creek Valley. Avoid the old trail—it is more direct but heavily eroded and slightly dangerous.

At a small saddle directly below the summit of Flattop, the old and new trails converge, and the steep final stretch begins. The trail remains well-marked but becomes rougher and more difficult than many people anticipate. Watch your footing, use your hands for balance if necessary, and take your time. Be especially careful of loose rock—with all the traffic on Flattop, any rocks you kick loose stand a chance of injuring someone below. Shout a warning call of "rock!" when you dislodge one, and keep an eye on the hikers above you. You'll also likely notice some

On Flattop Mountain (Photo courtesy of Chugach State Park)

litter, a growing problem on this heavily trafficked mountain. Please pack out everything you pack in.

As you clamber over the final rise and emerge onto the broad summit plateau, do not be surprised if you're greeted by a powerful gust of wind. Even sunny days see strong winds rolling over this peak, so have warm clothes on hand as you kick back and enjoy the view. You'll see the entire Anchorage Bowl, bounded by the gray shores of Cook Inlet. Denali and the Alaska Range gleam white far across the water. But best of all, directly beneath your feet is the hallowed summit of Flattop, welcoming its pilgrims by the hundreds.

29 | POWERLINE TRAIL

Powerline Pass
Distance: 2 to 12 miles
Elevation Gain: 0 to 1500 feet
Hiking Time: 1 to 7 hours
Hike Difficulty: easy
Terrain: established trail
High Point: 3550 feet
USGS Maps: Anchorage A-7, Anchorage A-8

Traversal to Indian
Distance: 11 miles (one-way traverse)
Elevation Gain: 1500 feet
Hiking Time: 5 to 8 hours
Hike Difficulty: moderate
Terrain: established trail
High Point: 3550 feet
USGS Maps: Anchorage A-7, Anchorage A-8, Seward D-7

You're likely to encounter hikers, bikers, and climbers of every stripe throughout the expansive South Fork Campbell Creek Valley. Yet even when teeming with people, this alpine playground retains a sense of space. Its main thoroughfare is the Powerline Trail, running 6 miles from Glen Alps to Powerline Pass, with small side trails splitting off every few miles. Come visit a high pass, tackle a nearby peak, or simply enjoy a few miles of fresh air and glimpse a moose or two.

Getting There: Glen Alps Trailhead. From downtown Anchorage, drive 7 miles south on the Seward Highway and take the O'Malley Road exit. Turn left (east) onto O'Malley and follow it toward the mountains for 3½ miles. Turn right onto Hillside Drive. Follow this road for 1 mile, and

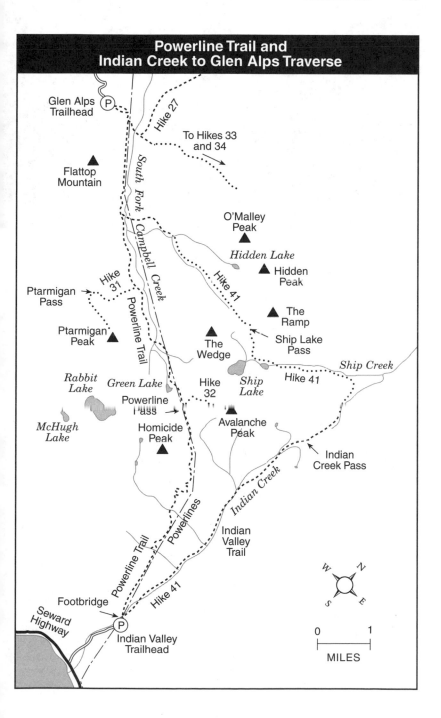

Powerline Trail and Indian Creek to Glen Alps Traverse

Glen Alps Trailhead (P)

Hike 27

To Hikes 33 and 34

Flattop Mountain

South Fork Campbell Creek

O'Malley Peak

Hidden Lake

Hidden Peak

Hike 31

Hike 41

Ptarmigan Pass

Powerline Trail

The Ramp

Ship Lake Pass

Ptarmigan Peak

The Wedge

Ship Creek

Rabbit Lake

Green Lake

Hike 32

Ship Lake

Hike 41

Powerline Pass

McHugh Lake

Homicide Peak

Avalanche Peak

Indian Creek Pass

Indian Creek

Powerlines

Indian Valley Trail

Powerline Trail

Footbridge

Hike 41

Seward Highway

(P) Indian Valley Trailhead

W N S E

0   1
MILES

The Powerline Trail

then turn left onto Upper Huffman Road. Continue ¾ mile and turn right onto Toilsome Hill Drive. A Chugach State Park sign marks this intersection. Follow Toilsome Hill (which soon becomes a dirt road) up several switchbacks for about 2 miles and turn left into the trailhead parking lot.

From the trailhead, follow signs directing you east toward the Powerline Trail. Take either of the two trails descending into the wooded valley: they meet again ¼ mile later in a large clearing. Here, turn right onto the Powerline Trail. This road-sized swath leads up the broad valley, paralleling a string of powerlines connecting Anchorage to the town of Indian. Though you can hike the entire length, most people make shorter out-and-back trips.

The Powerline Trail, always wide and clear but sometimes muddy, climbs slowly upvalley. As you hike, keep an eye out for pikas, marmots, moose, and the occasional Dall sheep. After 4½ miles, the trail passes a series of shimmering tarns. The largest of these, Green Lake, lies just beneath Powerline Pass. If you're out for a day hike, bring a lunch and stop here for a picnic. The trail becomes steeper after Green Lake, but stays wide and smooth enough to drive a truck to the pass. Avalanche Peak rises just north of the pass, and as you might suspect, the pass is prone to avalanches and should be avoided in the winter. In the hiking season, though, you can follow an easy route from Powerline Pass to Avalanche's summit (Hike 32).

The Powerline Trail also has a wealth of side trails. Within ½ mile of the trailhead, you'll pass a marked cut-off heading left to the Middle Fork Loop, the Williwaw Lakes Trail and The Ballpark, and O'Malley Peak (Hikes 27, 33, and 34). Two miles farther, a sign marks the trail to Hidden Lake and Ship Lake Pass (Hike 30). Another 1½ miles farther, a low point on the ridge to your right marks the steep climb to Ptarmigan Pass and Ptarmigan Peak (Hike 31). This pass also offers access to McHugh and Rabbit Lakes.

Heading east from Powerline Pass, the trail descends through switchbacks, entering the trees around mile 7. Shortly after mile 9 it crosses a large stream; be prepared to get your feet wet. At mile 11, the trail diverts from underneath the powerlines and into the woods, but quickly returns again. A little farther down, it diverts a second time—here it becomes a road, and shortly hits a gate. Don't follow this second diversion; instead, cross east underneath the powerlines and look for a smaller trail leading downhill to a footbridge over Indian Creek. The trailhead is 5 minutes farther.

30 | HIDDEN LAKE, THE RAMP, AND THE WEDGE

Hidden Lake
Distance: 9 miles
Elevation Gain: 1550 feet
Hiking Time: 5 to 7 hours
Hike Difficulty: easy
Terrain: established trail
High Point: 3650 feet
USGS Maps: Anchorage A-7, Anchorage A-8

The Ramp
Distance: 11 miles
Elevation Gain: 3100 feet
Hiking Time: 7 to 10 hours
Hike Difficulty: moderate
Terrain: alpine tundra, scree
High Point: 5240 feet
USGS Maps: Anchorage A-7, Anchorage A-8

The Wedge
Distance: 12 miles
Elevation Gain: 2500 feet
Hiking Time: 6 to 9 hours
Hike Difficulty: moderate
Terrain: established trail, alpine tundra
High Point: 4660 feet
USGS Maps: Anchorage A-7, Anchorage A-8

Just off the Powerline Trail, a narrow track leads up a side valley to a trio of grand destinations: Hidden Lake, The Ramp, and The Wedge. Each is worth a visit, and with an early start and enough energy you can see all three in the same day. Hidden Lake—so named because you will not see it until you've

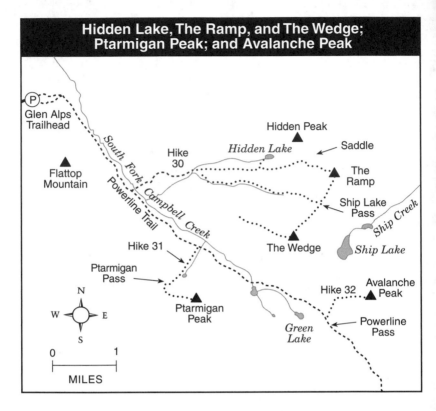

Hidden Lake, The Ramp, and The Wedge; Ptarmigan Peak; and Avalanche Peak

almost stepped in it—is the easiest of the three destinations. The Ramp, an elegant triangular peak rising above Ship Lake Pass, boasts a tiny summit and expansive vistas. The Wedge is altogether different, a crumbling mess of a mountain cleaving South Fork Campbell Creek Valley in two. It's worth a visit for precipitous views over both halves of the valley.

Getting There: Glen Alps Trailhead. From downtown Anchorage, drive 7 miles south on the Seward Highway and take the O'Malley Road exit. Turn left (east) onto O'Malley and follow it toward the mountains for 3½ miles. Turn right onto Hillside Drive. Follow this road for 1 mile, and then turn left onto Upper Huffman Road. Continue ¾ mile and turn right onto Toilsome Hill Drive. A Chugach State Park sign marks this intersection. Follow Toilsome Hill (which soon becomes a dirt road) up several switchbacks for about 2 miles and turn left into the trailhead parking lot.

From the trailhead, follow signs directing you east toward the Powerline Trail. Take either of the two trails descending into the wooded valley: they meet again ¼ mile later in a large clearing. Here, turn right onto the Powerline Trail. After following this trail for 2 miles, look for a sign marking a small trail on your left. Follow this side trail as it descends to meet

Campbell Creek. There's no bridge over the creek, but the crossing is not difficult. Bring extra socks or plan on continuing the hike with wet feet.

The trail continues through a muddy section on the far side of the creek and slowly climbs upvalley through stunted, windblown coniferous trees (called krumholz) characteristic of many subalpine areas in the park. A mile after crossing the creek, the trail crosses another, smaller creek. After this second creek, you'll reach a fork in the trail. Go right to reach Ship Lake Pass and The Wedge, or turn left for Hidden Lake and The Ramp.

The route to Hidden Lake follows the left fork and climbs along a small ridge. About a mile from the fork, you'll be nearly level with the cirque containing Hidden Lake (though you will not be able to see the lake—it's hidden, remember?). From here, turn north and cross the tundra to a small stream. Turn right and follow this stream up and over a small hill to the lake's rocky shores. Surrounded by towering slopes, Hidden Lake is truly secluded. A small mound obscures views of Anchorage, adding to the tarn's intimate feel.

To climb The Ramp, follow the left fork from the second stream crossing and climb along the small ridge up to a saddle between Hidden Peak and The Ramp. Turn right at the saddle and follow the ridge southeast for ½ mile until you are just below The Ramp's summit. The sheep trail peters

The Wedge

out here, and reaching the summit directly along the ridge involves a short scramble. Alternatively, traverse a short distance to the right onto the south face of The Ramp and trudge up a scree slope for the last 100 feet to the narrow summit. From The Ramp, return the way you came or descend south from the summit down a scree-covered ridge directly to Ship Lake Pass. (The Ramp can also be climbed from Ship Lake Pass, but the route described above avoids a tiresome trudge up scree slopes and offers better views along the way.)

To reach Ship Lake Pass and The Wedge, take the right fork at the second stream crossing. An ill-defined trail meanders up the center of the valley, but here on the high tundra you don't need much of a trail. Make your way up the valley floor for about 2 miles, aiming for the low saddle between The Ramp and The Wedge. Ship Lake Pass will mark the turnaround point for some, but it's only another 600 vertical feet to reach The Wedge. Turn right and climb up a broad, solid ridge to The Wedge's summit. You can venture a little farther on a small sheep trail that continues west along the top of several dramatic, crumbling pinnacles, but return to Ship Lake Pass for a safe descent.

31 | PTARMIGAN PEAK

Distance: 10 miles
Elevation Gain: 2700 feet
Hiking Time: 5 to 8 hours
Hike Difficulty: moderate
Terrain: alpine tundra, scree, scrambling
High Point: 4880 feet
USGS Maps: Anchorage A-7, Anchorage A-8

Ptarmigan Peak, a craggy pyramid rising behind popular Flattop Mountain, is perhaps the fiercest-looking mountain near Anchorage. Its most prominent feature, a steep north face perennially streaked white by a snow couloir, intimidates many would-be summiters. Despite this, the mountain actually makes for a pleasant visit. It's known among the outdoor community as a scenic challenge that beginning climbers should attempt before earning their "Chugach legs." The standard (and very safe) route avoids the couloir, instead climbing from the Powerline Trail past a windswept tarn, up scree slopes and a jumble of shallow gullies to the summit.

Getting There: Glen Alps Trailhead. From downtown Anchorage, drive 7 miles south on the Seward Highway and take the O'Malley Road exit. Turn left (east) onto O'Malley and follow it toward the mountains for 3½ miles. Turn right onto Hillside Drive. Follow this road for 1 mile, and then turn left onto Upper Huffman Road. Continue ¾ mile and turn right onto Toilsome Hill Drive. A Chugach State Park sign marks this intersection. Follow Toilsome Hill (which soon becomes a dirt road) up several switchbacks for about 2 miles and turn left into the trailhead parking lot.

From the trailhead, head to the Powerline Trail and turn east, joining the usual parade of mountain bikers, dog walkers, joggers, and the occasional moose. As you follow this well-worn trail, keep track of the mountains on your right. Several peaks dot the ridge: the first is Flattop, followed by two higher, unnamed peaks. After the second unnamed peak, the ridge drops significantly down to a wide saddle—Ptarmigan Pass.

After following along the Powerline Trail for 3 miles, you'll be just north of Ptarmigan Pass. Turn sharply right and ascend the brushy slopes, keeping west (right) of the creek flowing down from the pass. From atop the broad plateau, you'll have views across both Rabbit Creek and Powerline Pass Valleys. Even if you do not climb the peak, it's worth making a trip to the pass; in good weather it makes an excellent picnic site or high camp.

Ptarmigan Peak rises abruptly at the southeast edge of the pass. Head across the pass and up a small rise, gaining Ptarmigan's southwest ridge. Stick to this ridge, which climbs directly from the pass, until it steepens severely and the scree fields give way to a myriad of steep, shallow gullies. There is no obvious main route from this point, but nearly all of these gullies reach the summit (the westernmost of the two high points) a short distance above. Pick a gully that looks promising and expect a small amount of scrambling.

Views over Turnagain Arm, Rabbit Lake, and the Suicide Peaks will keep you lingering at the summit. Don't be surprised to see low-flying commercial jets making their final approach into Anchorage International Airport; the usual flight path takes them directly overhead. The

Ptarmigan Peak from Ptarmigan Pass

jet passengers, on the other hand, might be startled by the sight of *you* atop this dramatic and seemingly inaccessible peak.

32 | AVALANCHE PEAK

Distance: 14 miles
Elevation Gain: 2900 feet
Hiking Time: 8 to 10 hours
Hike Difficulty: moderate
Terrain: rough trail, scree
High Point: 5050 feet
USGS Maps: Anchorage A-7, Anchorage A-8

If you're eager to explore Campbell Creek Valley beyond the Powerline Trail, visit Avalanche Peak. Easily climbed from Powerline Pass, Avalanche's southern ridge offers a pleasant hike with little scree and no scrambling. The main drawback is the 6-mile approach hike; bike to the pass to save time, or plan for a long day. Also consider camping at Green Lake and summitting the next morning.

Getting There: Glen Alps Trailhead. From downtown Anchorage, drive 7 miles south on the Seward Highway and take the O'Malley Road exit. Turn left (east) onto O'Malley and follow it toward the mountains for 3½ miles. Turn right onto Hillside Drive. Follow this road for 1 mile, and then turn left onto Upper Huffman Road. Continue ¾ mile and turn right onto Toilsome Hill Drive. A Chugach State Park sign marks this intersection. Follow Toilsome Hill (which soon becomes a dirt road) up several switchbacks for about 2 miles and turn left into the trailhead parking lot.

From the trailhead, head to the Powerline Trail and turn east. Follow the main trail upvalley, avoiding side tracks. Five and one-half miles from Glen Alps lies Green Lake, an ideal camping spot. The pass is ½ mile beyond the lake, linking Campbell Creek and Indian Creek Valleys.

Avalanche is aptly named—this route heads up the mountain's southern slopes, which are perfectly angled to send dangerous snowslides down on Powerline Pass. Avoid the entire area during winter.

Once at Powerline Pass, turn left and begin climbing. You won't find a trail, but the footing on the tundra is solid. After gaining 1200 feet along the southern ridge, you'll approach a false summit. Here the route becomes less steep. Turn right and follow the gently sloping ridge for ¼ mile to Avalanche's high point. Most hikers will be comfortable on the ridge, but you can always find easier walking on the south side of the ridge and

Avalanche Peak

traverse past any difficult segments. Avalanche is a true walker's peak: the steep drop off the north side of the ridge adds some drama, but the route does not require any scrambling. At the summit are excellent views of Turnagain Arm, Ship Lake sparkling below Avalanche's steep northwest wall, and diminutive Flattop, 1500 feet below you at the far end of the valley.

33 | WILLIWAW LAKES TRAIL AND THE BALLPARK

Williwaw Lakes
Distance: 8 miles (full loop)
Elevation Gain: 1800 feet via The Ballpark; 600 feet via Williwaw Lakes Trail
Hiking Time: 5 to 7 hours
Hike Difficulty: moderate
Terrain: established trail, alpine tundra
High Point: 3750 feet
USGS Maps: Anchorage A-7, Anchorage A-8

The Williwaw Lakes, tucked high in a valley above East Anchorage, are a justifiably popular backpacking destination. Two trails lead to their shores: the gentle Williwaw Lakes Trail and the more rugged Ballpark trail. Hikers looking for an easy route to the lakes will want to use the Williwaw Lakes Trail, but a more interesting route makes a loop connecting The Ballpark to the Williwaw Lakes Trail as described below. While you can easily make a day trip to these pristine lakes, the valley is also great place to camp and explore. Possible side trips include climbs on O'Malley Peak and Mount Williwaw (Hikes 34 and 35).

Getting There: Glen Alps Trailhead. From downtown Anchorage, drive 7 miles south on the Seward Highway and take the O'Malley Road exit. Turn left (east) onto O'Malley and follow it toward the mountains for 3½ miles. Turn right onto Hillside Drive. Follow this road for 1 mile, and then turn left onto Upper Huffman Road. Continue ¾ mile and turn right onto Toilsome Hill Drive. A Chugach State Park sign marks this intersection. Follow Toilsome Hill (which soon becomes a dirt road) up several switchbacks for about 2 miles and turn left into the trailhead parking lot.

From the parking lot, head to the Powerline Trail and turn east. After following the Powerline Trail for ¼ mile, turn left at a sign marking the Middle Fork Loop Trail. Follow the trail down to Campbell Creek and cross on a footbridge. Shortly afterward, the trail forks, heading left on the Middle Fork Loop Trail and continuing straight on the unmarked Ballpark trail. (The park plans to reroute this section of the Middle Fork Loop Trail

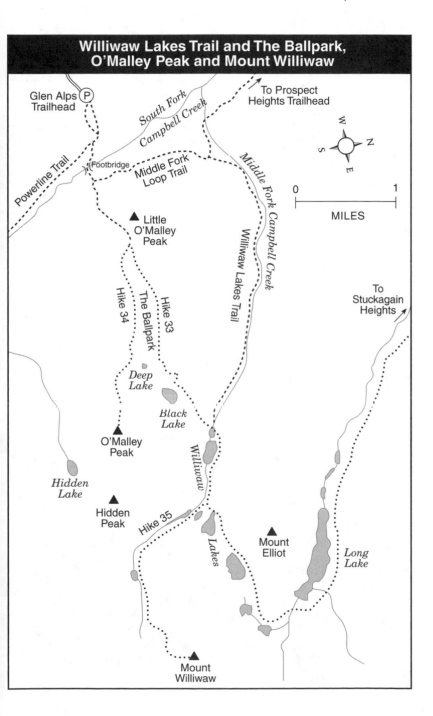

Williwaw Lakes Trail and The Ballpark, O'Malley Peak and Mount Williwaw

Glen Alps Trailhead

To Prospect Heights Trailhead

South Fork Campbell Creek

Powerline Trail

Footbridge

Middle Fork Loop Trail

Middle Fork Campbell Creek

Little O'Malley Peak

Williwaw Lakes Trail

0   1
MILES

Hike 34

The Ballpark

Hike 33

To Stuckagain Heights

Deep Lake

Black Lake

O'Malley Peak

Williwaw

Hidden Lake

Hidden Peak

Hike 35

Lakes

Mount Elliot

Long Lake

Mount Williwaw

and the easy route to Williwaw Lakes. Call ahead to find out the trail's current status.)

To reach the lakes via The Ballpark, follow the unmarked trail as it climbs a shallow gully. Sections can be muddy; please stick to the main route to minimize erosion. At the top of the gully is a small saddle, beyond which lies the vast Ballpark. This strange cirque, sloping gently toward Anchorage, is large enough to fit a ballpark for every team in the Major Leagues. The land's gentle undulations play tricks on your eyes: a distant hiker might suddenly disappear, only to reappear after cresting an imperceptible rise. The terrain, punctuated by dips and erratics, resembles a lichened moonscape.

Follow a trail east through The Ballpark. It forks after a short distance; follow the left fork, heading east and slightly north into the center of the cirque. Near The Ballpark's eastern edge sits Deep Lake, a small tarn below O'Malley Peak. Because of the strange shape of this land, you can't see Deep Lake until you're almost at its shore. O'Malley Peak, on the other hand, dominates the entire eastern horizon. The Ballpark is a great place to spend a night in the high country, weather permitting. Camp at Deep Lake and watch the sun set on the Alaska Range.

To reach the Williwaw Lakes, continue over the pass at The Ballpark's eastern edge. Descend down a steep, scree-filled gully. This can be tricky, so proceed with caution. In the gully, traverse north across scree to more solid ground along the gully's edge. Exit the bottom of the gully onto a flat bench. From here it is a short hike to Black Lake, hidden in the shadow of O'Malley's awesome north face, where snowmelt waters touch green shores on one side and rocks blackened by lichen on the other.

Spring views of Anchorage and Mount Susitna from The Ballpark

Descend along a faint trail from Black Lake to the Middle Fork Campbell Creek Valley floor. A trail of sorts leads northeast and intersects the Williwaw Lakes Trail at the first of the Williwaw Lakes. Continue east to explore the lakes. Mount Williwaw (Hike 35) and Long Lake (Hike 23) make for more lengthy and ambitious trips. Consider making a loop from Glen Alps to Stuckagain Heights via the Williwaw Lakes and North Fork Campbell Creek Valley, with potential side trips up Mount Williwaw and other peaks in the valley.

Otherwise, complete the loop back to Glen Alps (after at least a *little* exploration of the lakes!) by following the Williwaw Lakes Trail westward through Middle Fork Campbell Creek Valley. The gentle trail travels through low brush and exquisitely gnarled krumholz (wind-battered, stunted hemlocks) before intersecting the Middle Fork Loop Trail. Turn left at this intersection and return to Glen Alps. An easier walk than The Ballpark trail, the Williwaw Lakes Trail is also suitable as an out-and-back hike (from Glen Alps) for all levels of experience.

34 | O'MALLEY PEAK

Little O'Malley
Distance: 4 miles
Elevation Gain: 1200 feet
Hiking Time: 2 to 3 hours
Hike Difficulty: easy
Terrain: established trail
High Point: 3278 feet
USGS Map: Anchorage A-8

O'Malley Peak
Distance: 8 miles
Elevation Gain: 3100 feet
Hiking Time: 5 to 8 hours
Hike Difficulty: moderate
Terrain: alpine tundra, scree
High Point: 5150 feet
USGS Maps: Anchorage A-7, Anchorage A-8

Pinnacled and precipitous, O'Malley Peak towers above South Anchorage in dramatic relief. Wild and windy, exposed yet safe, and on the edge of town, the mountain should by all rights be crowded with hikers. But it remains a quiet place. Climb O'Malley in an afternoon or combine it with a longer trip to Williwaw Lakes. For a shorter outing, visit Little O'Malley,

Resting atop Little O'Malley. The Ballpark (right) and O'Malley Peak (left) are in the background.

perched at the end of O'Malley Peak's long western ridge. Much less traveled than neighboring Flattop Peak, Little O'Malley is a great climb for kids and less experienced hikers.

Getting There: Glen Alps Trailhead. From downtown Anchorage, drive 7 miles south on the Seward Highway and take the O'Malley Road exit. Turn left (east) onto O'Malley and follow it toward the mountains for 3½ miles. Turn right onto Hillside Drive. Follow this road for 1 mile, and then turn left onto Upper Huffman Road. Continue ¾ mile and turn right onto Toilsome Hill Drive. A Chugach State Park sign marks this intersection. Follow Toilsome Hill (which soon becomes a dirt road) up several switchbacks for about 2 miles and turn left into the trailhead parking lot.

From the trailhead, follow signs to the Powerline Trail and turn east. After ¼ mile, turn left at a sign marking the Middle Fork Loop Trail. Follow the trail down to Campbell Creek and cross a footbridge. Shortly past the bridge, the trail forks. The left fork leads to the Middle Fork Loop Trail, while the unmarked right fork (your route) heads up toward O'Malley Peak. O'Malley's makeshift trail resembles its makeshift name: known for years simply as "the mountain at the end of O'Malley Road" (itself named for an early homesteader), O'Malley's provisional name appears to have stuck.

The trail is muddy and eroded early on—try to stay on the main path to minimize further damage. It ascends a shallow gully and reaches a saddle after a short but strenuous climb. Beyond this saddle lies The Ballpark, a high, wide, and unusually flat cirque. To reach Little O'Malley Peak, turn left at the saddle and follow the ridge for ¼ mile. Here you'll find solitude and fine views of Anchorage.

To reach O'Malley Peak, follow a trail east through The Ballpark, paralleling O'Malley's western ridge (now on your right). Stay right when the trail forks, keeping near the ridge. After hiking for 1½ miles, you'll reach Deep Lake, a small and sunken tarn.

O'Malley rises steeply from Deep Lake, its west face marked by two prominent scree gullies. Hike up the shallower right gully, taking heed of loose rock. The slippery scree can be frustrating but soon ends at a small saddle between Point 4630 and O'Malley's summit. Don't get too excited, though: several false summits remain between you and the peak. Follow a faint Dall sheep trail leading northeast along the ridge. If you miss this trail, simply pick your way across O'Malley's southern slopes, working eastward and upward below the ridge crest. Follow the path of least resistance and you'll avoid unnecessary scrambling.

Continue for ½ mile along the ridge to O'Malley's summit. From here you'll have views of Anchorage and Chugach State Park, but the best view of all is straight down O'Malley's sheer north face. It drops, almost vertically, more than 2000 feet to shimmering Black Lake—not for the faint of heart!

35 | MOUNT WILLIWAW

Distance: 14 miles (6 miles round trip from the first of the Williwaw Lakes)
Elevation Gain: 3400 feet (2800 feet from Williwaw Lakes)
Hiking Time: 9 to 12 hours (3 to 5 hours from Williwaw Lakes)
Hike Difficulty: difficult
Terrain: scree
High Point: 5445 feet
USGS Maps: Anchorage A-7, Anchorage A-8

Mount Williwaw, partially tucked from view behind closer peaks, looks unremarkable from Anchorage. Yet it's the highest of the mountains rising behind the city, a massive pyramid whose true dominance over the landscape is best measured from its summit. This route is not easy, involving a long approach and the negotiation of a steep gully. It can be climbed from Glen Alps in a long day or as a challenging side trip for backpackers camped at the Williwaw Lakes.

Getting There: Glen Alps Trailhead. From downtown Anchorage, drive 7 miles south on the Seward Highway and take the O'Malley Road exit. Turn left (east) onto O'Malley and follow it toward the mountains for 3½ miles. Turn right onto Hillside Drive. Follow this road for 1 mile, and then turn left onto Upper Huffman Road. Continue ¾ mile and turn right onto Toilsome Hill Drive. A Chugach State Park sign marks this intersection. Follow Toilsome Hill (which soon becomes a dirt road) up several switchbacks for about 2 miles and turn left into the trailhead parking lot.

Follow signs to the Powerline Trail and, after heading east for ¼ mile, take the first left at a sign marking the Williwaw Lakes Trail. Descend to a footbridge across Campbell Creek. Shortly past this bridge, turn left and follow the muddy trail as it wraps around the base of Little O'Malley Peak. The trail quality gradually improves and after 4 miles

Winter on Mount Williwaw, with its southwest gully clearly visible

you will reach the first of the Williwaw Lakes. (You can also reach the lakes via The Ballpark; see Hike 33 for more detail.) From the lakes, follow the trail east along the valley floor. One mile past the first lake, a large headwall separates the upper Middle Fork Campbell Creek Valley into two branches. The left branch continues along the Williwaw Lakes, eventually reaching Long Lake; the route up Mount Williwaw lies in the right branch.

Follow the creek up this branch, past two small lakes. As you near the end of the valley, climb into a small cirque and look for a narrow gully angling north. The gully should be obvious, hemmed between steep mountain walls. Since the gully often contains snow until late summer, it's advisable to have an ice ax. If the gully is snow-free, this is a straighforward scramble. Climb along the sides of the gully, where less scree collects and handholds can be found for extra balance. Beware of rockfall. After gaining 900 feet in the gully, you'll emerge onto a wide scree slope angling more gently toward the summit. Rather than charging directly up this slope, traverse to your right, where you'll find better footing along Williwaw's southern ridge. Gain 700 feet along this uncomplicated ridge and you'll be standing on Chugach State Park's highest point west of Ship Creek.

If the season is late, come prepared for the mountain's namesake: williwaws are fierce, sudden windstorms that periodically sweep through these mountains. But if the weather is fine, lounge for a while. Sign the summit register and take in views of the iridescent Williwaw Lakes and the lights of Anchorage framed by the snow-capped peaks of the distant Alaska Range.

THE SOUTH PARK

Just as the western park is intertwined with Anchorage, the southern park is tied to the sea. Most of the hikes begin near the shores of Turnagain Arm, a constant sight from any high point in the area. Stop at one of several scenic overlooks, such as Beluga Point, Windy Corner, or Bird Point, and you might see beluga whales swimming in the Arm, or the twice-daily bore tide—a dramatic ridge of water rising as the strong incoming tide surges over the outgoing tide.

Situated where land meets sea, the southern park is, not surprisingly, a wet place. Weather systems commonly sweep up from the south and dump their precipitation upon the first line of mountains bordering Turnagain Arm. This means thick snows in the winter, a preponderance of rain in the summer, and lots of glaciers. The heavy precipitation also results in thicker vegetation. The coniferous forests lining the eastern half of Turnagain Arm, extensions of the Southeast Alaskan rain forest, are dense with undergrowth. This secludes the lowland walks beneath a forest canopy and gives fascinating transitions from rain forest to tundra as one climbs. It also makes off-trail travel difficult, as you'll face nearly impenetrable brush the moment you leave the path.

The Seward Highway runs along Turnagain Arm's north coast, providing access to all the trailheads in this part of the park. It's been designated a National Scenic Byway and is one of the most beautiful drives in the state. As a result, summer traffic on the Seward Highway runs thicker than the salmon in Alaska's streams. It's crowded with tourists heading to Portage and the Kenai Peninsula, fishermen preparing to try their luck against the Kenai River's salmon and the halibut of Resurrection Bay, and Anchoragites fleeing the city to vacation homes. Take your time and enjoy the scenery.

Many trails depart from the Seward Highway, some starting at well-developed trailheads, others at gravel turnouts. Some of the park's most popular areas are here, including the Bird Ridge Trail (great for early season hiking) and the heavily used trail to Crow Pass. Yet this is also home to some very wild areas, remote wilderness settings like Grizzly Bear Lake and Bird Creek Valley. Prepare yourself for rugged terrain, variable weather, and spectacular beauty.

Penguin Peak rising above Turnagain Arm

36 | TURNAGAIN ARM TRAIL AND TABLE ROCK

Turnagain Arm Trail (Potter to Windy Corner)
Distance: 9½ miles (one-way traverse)
Elevation Gain: 1200 feet
Hiking Time: 5 to 7 hours
Hike Difficulty: easy
Terrain: established trail
High Point: 950 feet
USGS Maps: Anchorage A-8, Seward D-7

Table Rock from McHugh Trailhead
Distance: 2 miles
Elevation Gain: 900 feet
Hiking Time: 1 to 2 hours
Hike Difficulty: moderate
Terrain: established trail, rough trail
High Point: 1083 feet
USGS Map: Anchorage A-8

As its name suggests, the Turnagain Arm Trail winds along the northern shore of Turnagain Arm, a long, narrow fjord. Originally known as the Old Johnson Trail, it once ran all the way from Knik to Girdwood. Now it runs from Potter Marsh (just south of Anchorage) to Windy Corner, meandering through stands of poplar, aspen, spruce, and birch. Dazzling views across Turnagain Arm punctuate long stretches of dense forest, making for an enjoyable contrast. Near McHugh Wayside, a ½-mile side trail climbs to Table Rock, with high vistas and an excellent picnic spot. You can hike the Turnagain Arm Trail in its entirety (the mileposts count upward heading east) or start from any of four trailheads for shorter trips.

Getting There: The Turnagain Arm Trail

There are four trailheads: Potter at the western end of the trail, McHugh and Rainbow in the middle, and Windy Corner at the eastern end. Reach all of them by driving south from Anchorage on the Seward Highway.

Potter is on the left at mile 115.1, just past Chugach State Park Headquarters in the Potter Section House. A sign indicates the turn into the parking lot immediately off the highway, where you'll also find a viewing deck over the marsh. The large upper lot has displays about plate tectonics and the history of the railroad, plus a telescope pointing toward Mount Susitna across Cook Inlet.

McHugh Creek State Wayside is on the left at mile 111.7. Come to this trailhead for excellent picnic facilities, or to climb Table Rock. The

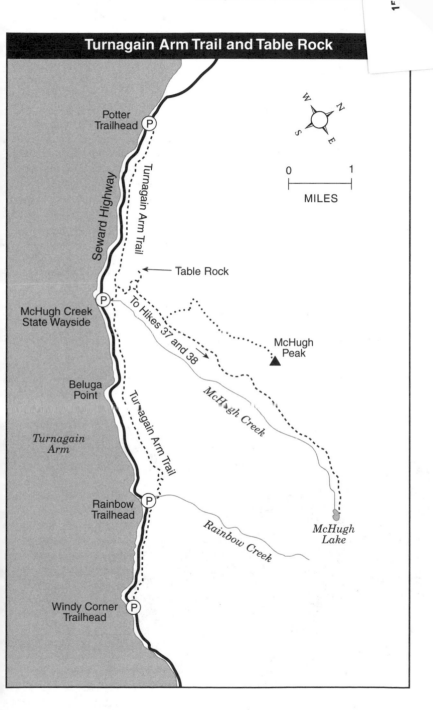

Turnagain Arm Trail and Table Rock

Potter
Trailhead

Seward Highway

Turnagain Arm Trail

Table Rock

To Hikes 37 and 38

McHugh Creek
State Wayside

McHugh
Peak

Beluga
Point

Turnagain Arm Trail

McHugh Creek

Turnagain
Arm

Rainbow
Trailhead

Rainbow Creek

McHugh
Lake

Windy Corner
Trailhead

0   1
MILES

Turnagain Arm Trail passes both the upper and lower parking lots.

Rainbow is at mile 108.3. Look for a turnout to the left with a large parking lot. No facilities here.

Windy Corner, at mile 106.7, is little more than a wide spot in the highway. Look for signs marking a pullout, and tourists gawking at Dall sheep on the cliffs above.

Cut from the brush and blasted from rock, the Turnagain Arm Trail has seen many uses. Built in 1910 to carry a telegraph line, it served as the main winter route from Seward to points north when avalanche danger made Crow and Indian Creek Passes impassable. Later, it provided an access corridor to workers constructing the Alaska railroad. Abandoned for years until Chugach State Park renovated it in the 1980s, it's now a popular trail. Come during full and new moons to see the tidal bore at full strength. Tidal bores occur in bays and inlets with extreme tidal fluctuations—Turnagain Arm boasts the second largest in the world, behind the Bay of Fundy in Nova Scotia. In a tidal bore, the incoming tide builds to a flood that overpowers the outgoing tide. The resulting tide resembles a wall of water ranging from several inches to several feet high.

Turnagain Arm and the Kenai Peninsula seen from Table Rock

The 3½-mile long section of the Turnagain Arm Trail that runs from Potter to McHugh Creek Wayside is largely flat, passing through predominantly deciduous forest. Check out Potter's graveled Nature Loop, lined with information on the plant life of the area. After a short distance it joins the main trail, which narrows to a track and heads over gently rolling hills to McHugh Wayside. After 3 miles, the trail intersects the McHugh/Rabbit Lakes Trail (Hike 37). Turn left here to visit Table Rock (described below). A little further, turn right at a signpost to reach McHugh Wayside's upper parking lot, or continue straight ahead to reach McHugh Creek. From here you can hike out to the lower McHugh parking lot or cross the creek and continue to Rainbow.

The 4 miles from McHugh Creek Wayside to Rainbow is somewhat rougher. Past McHugh, the trail gains several hundred feet of elevation and then skirts beneath cliffs. (This is a great chance to see how mountain goats live.) Soon the trail returns to the woods, where you'll find several brushy sections. Around mile 6 the trail begins a descent through elegant stands of birch to Rainbow Trailhead. This is arguably the most pleasant section of the entire trail; if you're short on time, park at Rainbow and hike a mile or so westward for a taste of the woods.

The trail deteriorates slightly over the 2 miles from Rainbow to Windy Corner, but offers more consistent views. On the descent to Windy Corner, watch for a prominent but unmarked right turn. At this intersection, a rough trail appears to continue straight ahead, but it soon deposits you on a steep scree slope with no easy way down. The correct trail turns right and descends through switchbacks to the highway.

For high views, visit Table Rock, a prominent outcropping perched 1000 feet above McHugh Wayside. To get there, start at the McHugh upper parking area and head west on the Turnagain Arm Trail. After ¼ mile you'll reach a T intersection with the McHugh/Rabbit Lakes Trail. (You'll also hit this intersection when hiking the Turnagain Arm Trail from Potter to McHugh Wayside; Table Rock makes a pleasant side trip.) Follow the McHugh/Rabbit Lakes Trail for about ¼ mile, and then turn left on a branching trail marked "scenic loop." Follow this trail as it meanders across the hillside. As it loops back toward the McHugh/Rabbit Lakes Trail, look for a side trail leading directly uphill (which should now be on your left) along the right edge of several large outcroppings. Follow this narrow track uphill until you reach a large spruce that has fallen across the trail and been cut out by a chain saw. Pass between the two halves and then immediately bend left onto Table Rock. Pay attention to your route—it can be confusing on the descent, and bushwhacking down McHugh's southern slopes would certainly ruin your day. Upon returning to the scenic loop, turn left and continue for several hundred feet to the McHugh/Rabbit Lakes Trail. Here turn right and head downhill, back to the Turnagain Arm Trail.

37 | McHugh/Rabbit Lakes Trail

Distance: 12 miles
Elevation Gain: 3100 feet
Hiking Time: 6 to 9 hours
Hike Difficulty: moderate
Terrain: established trail, alpine tundra
High Point: 3100 feet
USGS Maps: Anchorage A-7, Anchorage A-8

The McHugh/Rabbit Lakes Trail climbs steadily through mixed forests, high grasslands, and open tundra to McHugh and Rabbit Lakes, two azure tarns walled by steep mountains. The trail starts near sea level and gains considerable elevation, but it does so at a gentle grade. It's a manageable out-and-back day trip, but Rabbit and McHugh Lakes abound in beautiful (and popular) camping spots. Consider spending a night under the stars and exploring the lake environs the next day.

Getting There: McHugh Creek State Wayside. Drive south approximately 25 miles from downtown Anchorage on the Seward Highway. At mile 111.7, turn left into the McHugh Wayside parking area. The recently remodeled wayside now boasts a wealth of picnic tables, barbeque pits, parking spaces, and interpretive displays, all within a peaceful wooded setting beside McHugh Creek. Even if you're not planning on hiking, stop by to check out the impressive facilities. When setting off into the woods, keep in mind that the gate across the upper parking area closes at 9:00 P.M.—don't let your car get trapped inside.

From the highest parking area, follow the lone trail leading north into the woods. It soon intersects the Turnagain Arm Trail. Turn left and continue a short distance to an intersection, where a sign indicates the McHugh/Rabbit Lakes Trail leading off to the right. Just ¼ mile up this trail, a sign marks a "scenic loop" leading to Table Rock (see Hike 36). Bear right and continue on the main trail, which is marked with mileposts all the way to Rabbit Lake.

The trail climbs through wooded switchbacks for 1 mile, then emerges from the trees onto a grassy hillside high above McHugh Creek. A broad gully to the north leads up to McHugh Peak (Hike 38). The trail continues east across McHugh Peak's lower slopes for several miles, alternating between high grass and stunted trees. After another set of switchbacks, around mile 4, the trail climbs into alpine tundra. Brilliantly black, yellow, and white lichens, colorful lowbush berries, and glacial erratics (large boulders deposited willy-nilly across the valley floor by a retreating glacier) make for a captivating landscape. Near mile 5, a side trail leads to McHugh Lake; the main trail ends ½ mile later at Rabbit Lake,

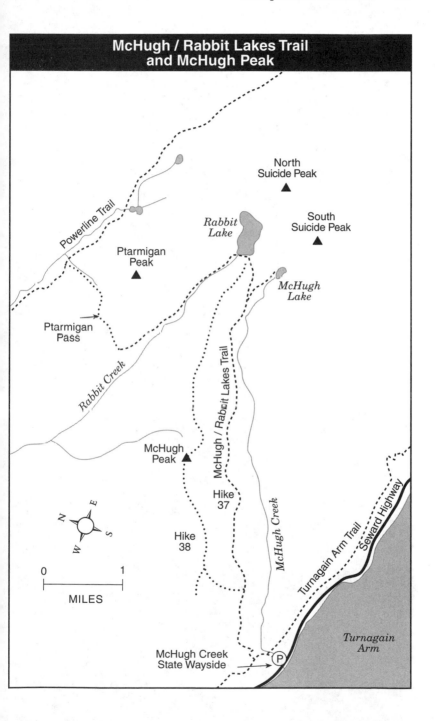

McHugh / Rabbit Lakes Trail and McHugh Peak

Powerline Trail

North Suicide Peak ▲

South Suicide Peak ▲

Rabbit Lake

Ptarmigan Peak ▲

McHugh Lake

Ptarmigan Pass

Rabbit Creek

McHugh / Rabbit Lakes Trail

McHugh Peak ▲

Hike 37

Hike 38

McHugh Creek

Turnagain Arm Trail

Seward Highway

N E S W

0   1

MILES

McHugh Creek State Wayside → Ⓟ

Turnagain Arm

nestled below the sheer faces of North and South Suicide Peaks.

Dry ground, plentiful water, and towering peaks make the area surrounding the lakes an excellent place to set up camp. From here, you can climb the 5000-foot Suicide Peaks (Hike 39) or McHugh Peak (via its eastern ridge, Hike 38). Either trip involves a half-day excursion from the lakes. If the weather is nice, you may well be content to lounge at the lakes, studying their contrast with the drab grays and blacks of the surrounding rocks.

On the McHugh/Rabbit Lakes Trail, beneath South Suicide Peak

38 | McHugh Peak

Distance: 7 miles (depending on route, see below)
Elevation Gain: 4200 feet
Hiking Time: 5 to 7 hours
Hike Difficulty: moderate to difficult
Terrain: established trail, scree, alpine tundra
High Point: 4301 feet
USGS Maps: Anchorage A-7, Anchorage A-8

Rising in a great massif from McHugh Creek Valley, McHugh Peak is not so much a distinct mountain as a 5-mile long ridge punctuated by craggy pinnacles. Though it borders south Anchorage, it lacks both the ease of access and the crowds you'll find at neighboring Flattop Mountain. Getting to the ridge crest involves a tiring climb, but easy walking atop the ridge—which overlooks South Anchorage and Turnagain Arm—rewards the effort.

Getting There: McHugh Creek State Wayside. Drive south approximately 25 miles from downtown Anchorage on the Seward Highway. At mile 111.7, turn left into McHugh Wayside parking area.

From the upper parking lot, turn left on the Turnagain Arm Trail. After ¼ mile, turn right on the McHugh/Rabbit Lakes Trail and begin climbing through several switchbacks. After 1½ miles, you'll emerge from the woods onto brushy slopes high above McHugh Creek. Here, look for a prominent gully coming down from the ridge on your left. Several paths should be visible from where you stand on the trail. Follow any one of these straight north, climbing through patchy brush and pebbly slopes toward the top of the gully. This is tedious work, a 1500-foot trudge up loose scree.

Once you reach the top, however, the rest of the climb is wonderful—a breezy walk with solid footing and excellent views. Follow the ridge crest northeast for 2 miles, traversing to the north around any difficult spots, to the small summit pinnacle. Jutting slightly higher than neighboring points, it seems determined to resist the inevitable fate of this mountain—to be slowly ground to silt and washed into Turnagain Arm.

You can either retrace your steps and return to McHugh Creek Trailhead, or continue for 3 more miles along the broad summit ridge as it gradually descends toward Rabbit Lake. From here, return to the trailhead via the McHugh/Rabbit Lakes Trail, an ambitious 12-mile round-trip loop. Reverse the direction of this loop and you can avoid trudging up the scree gully.

You can also climb McHugh from Glen Alps. Hike the Powerline Trail to Ptarmigan Pass. Cross over the pass and descend into Rabbit Creek Valley, then aim for McHugh's gentle north slopes directly across the valley

The summit pinnacle of McHugh Peak

floor. Firm ground and open terrain make this an ideal place to roam. It's a 16-mile hike from Glen Alps to the peak and back.

However you climb McHugh, bring water—none is available on the rocky ridge crest.

39 NORTH SUICIDE PEAK

From Rabbit Lake
Distance: 3 miles
Elevation Gain: 1900 feet
Hiking Time: 3 to 6 hours
Hike Difficulty: difficult
Terrain: scree, scrambling
High Point: 5065 feet
USGS Map: Anchorage A-7

Viewed from the shores of frigid Rabbit Lake, the Suicide Peaks live up to their name. They look so terrifying that—according to the early railroad workers who spied them from the tent city of Anchorage—you'd have to be suicidal to try to climb them. The climb is not easy, but anyone comfortable scrambling up scree slopes shouldn't be put off by the morose name.

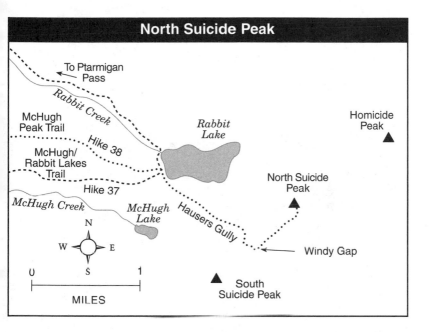

Both North and South Suicide can be climbed from Windy Gap, the high saddle splitting the peaks. North Suicide, the higher of the two peaks, offers more solid footing and is the more compelling climb. South Suicide is more often climbed from Falls Creek via its south ridge (Hike 40). The route up North Suicide from Rabbit Lake is described below.

Getting There: McHugh Creek State Wayside. Drive south 25 miles from downtown Anchorage on the Seward Highway. At mile 111.7, turn left into the McHugh Wayside parking area (see the McHugh/Rabbit Lakes Trail map).

From the upper parking lot, turn left on the Turnagain Arm Trail. After ¼ mile, turn right and follow the McHugh/Rabbit Lakes Trail for 5½ miles to Rabbit Lake, where excellent campsites abound. If the weather cooperates, watch the setting summer sun cast a brilliant pink and yellow alpenglow across the Suicide Peaks. From Rabbit Lake, hike southeast across the tundra to the rocky slopes below Windy Gap. Look for a large scree chute spilling down from the right edge of Windy Gap. This is Hausers Gully, named in honor of William Hauser, an eminent local climber who edited *30 Hikes in Alaska*, the state's first hiking guidebook.

Your route heads straight up Hausers Gully. It is fairly steep and loose scree makes the going difficult. Stick to the sides of the gully, where larger rocks provide better footing and the gully walls offer occasional handholds. Watch out for rockfall, a constant hazard. To avoid excess climbing, leave Hausers Gully when you draw level with Windy Gap and traverse to your

North Suicide Peak rises steeply from Windy Gap, as seen from South Suicide Peak.

left across a rocky face. This requires a short distance of difficult scrambling. If you'd rather skip the scrambling, follow the gully another 200 vertical feet or so to its upper end on South Suicide's north ridge and then descend the ridge to Windy Gap.

Windy Gap lives up to its name. Tucked high above Rabbit Lake between two massive piles of rock and snow, it funnels winds off Turnagain Arm through a notch no wider than a football field. Bring a warm hat and jacket on even the sunniest of days. From Windy Gap, turn left and begin climbing North Suicide's south ridge. After gaining several hundred feet in elevation, the ridge bends left and heads toward a false summit. Past the false summit, the ridge presents a short stretch of scrambling. Stay to the left of the ridge crest for mostly solid footing. Just past this point lies the summit, a full 1000 feet above Windy Gap. The views from this craggy height are thrilling, especially of luminous Rabbit Lake and South Suicide Peak—so close you can hear gusts of wind sweeping over its summit.

40 | FALLS CREEK TRAIL AND SOUTH SUICIDE PEAK

Falls Creek Tarn
Distance: 5 miles
Elevation Gain: 2900 feet
Hiking Time: 4 to 5 hours
Hike Difficulty: moderate
Terrain: established trail, rough trail
High Point: 3920 feet
USGS Maps: Anchorage A-7, Seward D-7

South Suicide Peak
Distance: 9 miles
Elevation Gain: 5000 feet
Hiking Time: 6 to 9 hours
Hike Difficulty: moderate to difficult
Terrain: rough trail, scree
High Point: 5005 feet
USGS Maps: Anchorage A-7, Seward D-7

Falls Creek tumbles down an intimate valley, cut off from the outside world by steep mountainsides. At the head of the valley you'll find Falls Creek Tarn, nestled beneath South Suicide Peak. The Falls Creek Trail follows the

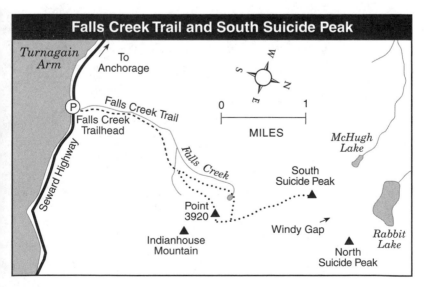

Falls Creek Trail and South Suicide Peak

creek from Turnagain Arm to the tarn, an inviting route to both the isolated lake and the mountain beyond. Come up for a picnic, explore the valley, and climb the peak, all in a comfortable day's hike.

Getting There: Falls Creek Trailhead. Head south out of Anchorage on the Seward Highway. One mile past Windy Corner (where tourists often gather to watch Dall sheep), look for a small pullout on the north side of the road. It's marked by a hiking sign at mile 105.6. The trailhead is small but sufficient for the surprisingly few visitors.

The trail leads straight into the woods from the pullout and, like nearly all hikes starting from the Seward Highway, heads uphill without delay. Within seconds the roar of speeding cars fades into the stillness of dense lowland forests. The thick brush can be troublesome where the trail narrows; wear long pants to protect against encroaching devil's club and bloodthirsty mosquitoes.

The trail splits ¼ mile from the trailhead. Both branches lead up the valley, but the left branch, which stays near the creek, involves a nightmare of overgrowth. Take the right-hand path. After another ½ mile the trail branches again. Follow the sign marked "trail" and head left, even though this fork appears less used. It leads downhill to the creek, then bends right and continues up the valley.

After about 1½ miles you'll leave tree line behind. Just ahead, Falls Creek Valley divides into two upper valleys. The right hand valley dead-ends in the abrupt rock faces of Indianhouse Mountain; the main trail heads into the left-hand valley, where you'll find Falls Creek Tarn. Cross the small tributary stream trickling down from the right-hand valley, then head left and follow the trail along the left fork of Falls Creek. The trail soon diverts from the stream and climbs a short distance before petering out at the base of a ridge below Point 3920. To reach Falls Creek Tarn, climb several hundred feet higher on the ridge, then traverse along clear slopes above the creek. Return to the creek when you're past all the brush. The tarn is just ahead, hidden from view.

For a less direct but more exciting trip to the tarn, follow a loop over Point 3920. Proceed to where the main trail peters out, then veer right and continue straight up the ridge along a sheep trail toward Point 3920. Occasional cairns mark the way; if you lose the sheep trail simply head steadily uphill along the ridge crest. The footing is solid for the most part, though a bit of scrambling is necessary. Point 3920 sits atop a steep rock wall rising from the tarn—don't lean over too far while gazing at the abrupt 900-foot drop! From this high point, carefully scramble down to the north until you reach a saddle just above the tarn. From here it is an easy descent to Falls Creek.

Falls Creek Tarn need not mark the end of your trip, however. A broad ridge rises from the lake toward South Suicide Peak, only 1½ miles away.

Falls Creek tumbling alongside the Falls Creek Trail

Climb to the pass above the tarn and follow the ridge leading northwest. With a relatively gentle grade and solid footing, the walking is pleasant— far more so than what you'll find on the steep route up South Suicide from Rabbit Lake. The summit views are excellent, particularly of nearby North Suicide Peak and the lakes below.

41 | INDIAN CREEK TO GLEN ALPS TRAVERSE

Indian Creek Pass
Distance: 10 miles
Elevation Gain: 2000 feet
Hiking Time: 5 to 7 hours
Hike Difficulty: moderate
Terrain: established trail
High Point: 2400 feet
USGS Maps: Anchorage A-7, Seward D-7

Traverse to Glen Alps
Distance: 15 miles (one-way traverse)
Elevation Gain: 3900 feet
Hiking Time: 10 to 14 hours (or overnight)
Hike Difficulty: moderate to difficult
Terrain: established trail, alpine tundra, scree, backcountry
High Point: 4000 feet
USGS Maps: Anchorage A-7, Anchorage A-8, Seward D-7

If Chugach State Park has a specific birthplace, it is Indian Creek Valley. In 1969, a petition to log the valley's towering old-growth spruce spurred a group of citizens to action. They sought to protect not only this valley, but the whole of Anchorage's vast backyard by campaigning for a state park. The park they proposed was larger than any ever created by a state, nearly two-thirds the size of Yosemite National Park. Backed by a coalition of local groups and widespread public support, they prevailed. Indian Valley is testament to their achievement: it remains, as it was then, a serene and pristine slice of Alaska's wilderness. (See Hike 29 for a map of the area.)

Getting There: Indian Valley Trailhead. From downtown Anchorage, drive south on the Seward Highway. At mile 103.1, just past the Indian Road intersection, turn left onto a dirt road named Ocean View Drive, immediately before the Turnagain House Restaurant. Slow down and look carefully; this turn is easy to miss. The road skirts the restaurant parking lot and

Ship Lake, the headwaters of Ship Creek

continues into the woods. After ½ mile, bear right at an intersection marked by a Chugach State Park sign. This road ends ¾ mile later at the trailhead.

Two paths lead from the trailhead. Ignore the left-hand trail crossing a bridge (Hike 29, which climbs steadily to Powerline Pass), and take the Indian Valley Trail, which heads uphill to the north. Wide and free of brush, it crosses Indian Creek several times on sturdy bridges. Tall conifers, spared destruction three decades ago, dominate the lowlands. Alder becomes more frequent as you gain elevation.

The trail climbs steadily, maintaining a gentle grade most of the way to Indian Creek Pass. Higher up, sections may be overgrown with tall grasses. The pass, less a distinct point than a mile-wide alpine plateau of tundra and low brush dividing the Ship Creek and Indian Creek watersheds, can be marshy and bug-ridden in places. The trail dwindles above tree line; look for broken sections of worn tundra and tall orange stakes planted at irregular intervals.

From the pass, you can retrace your steps to Indian, continue north for the 21-mile trek to Arctic Valley (Hike 22), or make a traverse to Glen Alps via Ship Lake Pass. This latter route requires some backcountry travel and makes an ideal overnight trip (or an ambitious day hike). Continue north from Indian Creek Pass for roughly 1 mile, then hook sharply southwest into a major side valley. Follow the headwaters of Ship Creek for 2 miles up the flat valley floor to Ship Lake. You likely won't find much of a trail, but follow the stream and you shouldn't lose your bearings. Ship Lake, surrounded by mile-high peaks, makes a magnificent campsite.

Fill up on water at Ship Lake and begin the steep, 1300-foot climb to Ship Lake Pass. Before charging up the hill in Rooseveltian fashion, make sure you're aiming for the right pass: head northwest toward the high pass, not southwest toward the lower pass between Avalanche Peak and The Wedge. It's a bit of a trudge, but once at the pass, your climbing is done—unless, of course, you're seized by a desire to climb The Wedge or The Ramp, both easily reached from here (Hike 30). Otherwise, continue west over the pass and descend along a small trail worn into the valley floor. After 2 miles you'll reach a stream and intersect a more prominent trail. Cross the stream and follow this trail west and south to Campbell Creek, which you'll have to ford. Just beyond the creek's western bank you'll reach the unmistakable Powerline Trail. Turn right and continue 2 more miles to Glen Alps Trailhead. You'll need to arrange for a pickup, or leave a car at Glen Alps to return to Indian.

One can, of course, complete this traverse in the opposite direction, starting at Glen Alps. This involves 1800 fewer feet of climbing but is a bit anticlimactic, hitting the high point early on. Furthermore, hikers starting at Glen Alps must descend the steep scree slope from Ship Lake Pass to Ship Lake, which is certainly less tiring but perhaps more difficult (given the steepness of the descent) than climbing *to* the pass, especially with a heavy pack.

42 | BIRD RIDGE

Point 3505
Distance: 5 miles
Elevation Gain: 3400 feet
Hiking Time: 3 to 5 hours
Hike Difficulty: moderate
Terrain: established trail
High Point: 3505 feet
USGS Maps: Anchorage A-7, Seward D-7

Bird Ridge Overlook
Distance: 13 miles
Elevation Gain: 5500 feet
Hiking Time: 7 to 10 hours
Hike Difficulty: moderate to difficult
Terrain: alpine tundra
High Point: 4650 feet
USGS Maps: Anchorage A-7, Seward D-7

Bird Ridge is an ideal introduction to the rigors and rewards of hiking in Chugach State Park. After a steep ascent to tree line, views of Turnagain Arm and the park's wild interior come quickly and dramatically. Due to its southern exposure, Bird Ridge emerges early from its winter hibernation, attracting spring hikers while surrounding mountains remain blanketed by snow. Expect to see plenty of other hikers enjoying the sunny evenings.

Getting There: Bird Ridge Trailhead. From Anchorage, drive south on the Seward Highway for 22½ miles. Bird Ridge Trailhead is at mile 102, just past the town of Indian. A sign marks the trailhead parking lot on the left side of the highway.

This recently renovated trailhead has ample parking and a ¼-mile paved interpretive trail recounting the history of the Alaska Railroad and stories of the indigenous Dena'ina people. The trail ends at a viewpoint overlooking Turnagain Arm. Here are two immaculate outhouses, specimens of rare beauty.

The trail to Point 3505 begins at these outhouses, where the pavement ends. The next 1½ miles, which climb steeply, are the toughest of the entire hike. Don't get discouraged! The views from above are breathtaking. Several flat stretches along the trail provide rest stops or turnaround points for less ambitious hikers, but the real prize lies another mile ahead.

Point 3505 (more a bump in the ridge than a peak) marks the turn-

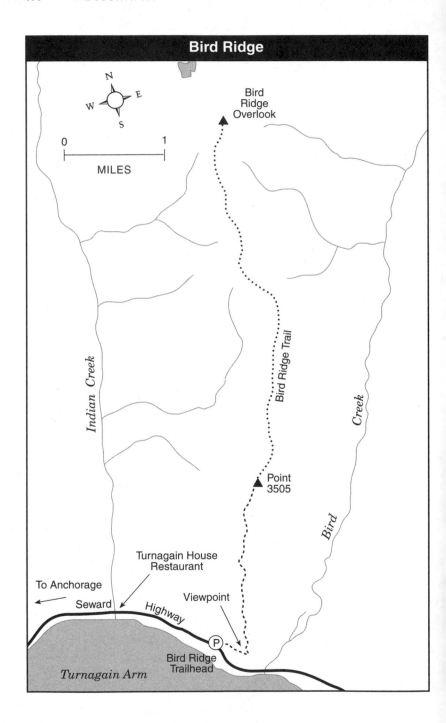

around for most hikers. It is also the finish line for the annual Robert Spurr Memorial Run, where intrepid competitors race from the trailhead (in a "shotgun and Jägermeister" start) in as little as 40 minutes. Hopefully you'll take a bit longer, smelling the abundant wildflowers along the way. Watch for bald eagles and, if your timing is right, bore tides in Turnagain Arm.

Now that the tough climbing is over, consider exploring the hauntingly barren upper ridge. It culminates at Bird Ridge Overlook 4 miles to the north. Even if you only go the first mile, you'll be struck by the stark elegance of this windswept landscape.

Past Point 3505, the trail quickly narrows to a sheep path. However, it remains level and easy to follow. The ridge rises to a knob, drops to a small saddle, and finally climbs steeply to the summit of Bird Ridge Overlook. At the saddle just below the overlook, divert from the sheep trail and head straight up the ridge toward the peak. The last 700 feet may require some easy scrambling. From the top, you'll see the headwaters of Ship Creek in the rugged valley 2000 feet below, the silty gray waters of Turnagain Arm behind you, and mountains unfolding in every direction on the horizon.

Bird Ridge and Turnagain Arm

43 PENGUIN PEAK

Distance: 6 miles
Elevation Gain: 4200 feet
Hiking Time: 4 to 6 hours
Hike Difficulty: moderate
Terrain: rough trail, alpine tundra
High Point: 4305 feet
USGS Map: Seward D-7

It is impossible to drive along the Seward Highway and not notice Penguin Peak, the hulking mountain dominating Turnagain Arm west of Girdwood. It frustrates motorists with highway-closing avalanches in the winter, and slows traffic in the summer when tourists stop to watch Dall sheep prance across its rocky cliffs. But relatively few people know Penguin Peak for the gentle route up its western slopes and the sweeping views over Turnagain Arm from its upper ridge. Once at this high outpost you'll quickly forget about the traffic jams far below.

Getting There: Bird Creek Valley Trailhead. Drive south on the Seward Highway out of Anchorage. Continue past Bird Creek and nearby Bird Creek Recreation Site. One-half mile farther, turn left on Konikson Road, just past a gas station. Follow this nondescript dirt road for ½ mile to where it dead-ends in a large gravel parking area. Chugach State Park signs mark the trailhead.

Start your hike on a wide dirt road leading into the dense forest. As the lush undergrowth attests, Bird Creek Valley is part of the northernmost extension of boreal rain forest in North America, receiving up to 120 inches of average annual precipitation. Many trails still crisscross this valley from logging projects during Anchorage's frontier days. In keeping with the park's multi-use mandate, expect to share these trails with ATVs and bikers during the summer and snow machines in winter. Also, gold panning is allowed in Bird Creek between March 16 and July 14—bring a pan and let your Alaskan prospecting dreams run wild.

About a hundred yards past the trailhead, the dirt road splits. Follow the right fork for ½ mile to the first sizable trail heading sharply to your right. Note the broad summit of Penguin Peak framed between the trees on each side of the trail and the obvious stream valley cutting down the western slopes of the mountain—that's your staircase to the top. The ascent begins at the base of a wide avalanche runout. This chute does not avalanche every winter, but when it does a tremendous roar is heard for miles, and an impressive snow pile will remain beside the trail throughout the summer.

The trail narrows quickly as it ascends alongside a usually dry streambed.

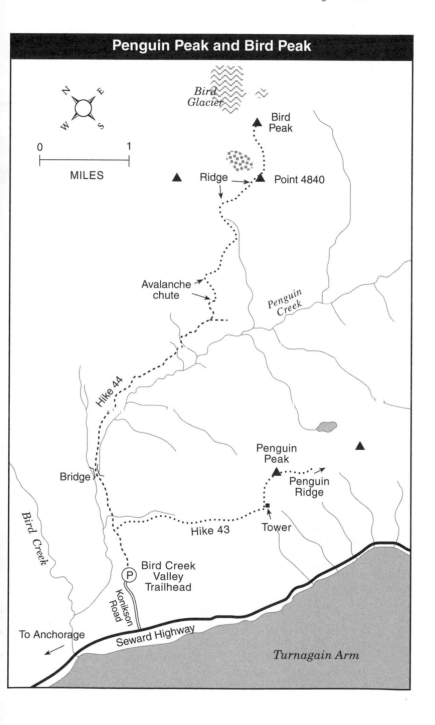

Penguin Peak and Bird Peak

Bird Glacier

Bird Peak

Ridge

Point 4840

Avalanche chute

Penguin Creek

Hike 44

Bridge

Penguin Peak

Penguin Ridge

Hike 43

Tower

Bird Creek

Bird Creek Valley Trailhead

Konikson Road

To Anchorage

Seward Highway

Turnagain Arm

N E W S

0 1
MILES

Travel becomes more difficult as you move higher and the alders thicken. Eventually only the remnants of a trail guide you uphill. This is enough, though. If you keep close to the streambed and follow the path of least resistance, you can largely avoid bushwhacking. The trail improves with elevation and you'll soon reach open tundra.

After emerging from the brushy stream valley, continue southeast across a meadow colored with bluebells and lupine, then up a short rise to a plateau. Here a large radio tower mars the otherwise beautiful vista. Carefully approach the edge of the plateau on your right and stop at this lookout point. High cliffs rise along the entire length of Turnagain Arm and this spot offers particularly awe-inspiring views. As you approach the edge you'll find yourself poised almost directly above the highway, looking down more than 3000 feet to a string of cars creeping alongside the mud flats of Turnagain Arm.

Once finished surveying the lowlands, turn around and hike the last 1000 feet to the summit of Penguin Peak. Gain the ridge just north of the plateau and follow this to the visible false summit. Here a large cairn hides a misplaced summit register with entries dating back to 1976. Don't be fooled: the true high point lies a short hop eastward. The grassy summit, marked by a cairn containing the true summit register, is perfect for lounging or picnicking. If it's clear, you'll see popular Bird Ridge to the west and Bird Peak (unconnected to the ridge) looming directly north across alder-choked Penguin Creek Valley.

If you have more time at your disposal, you may want to continue eastward along the ridge past Penguin Peak. It's possible, though not easy, to follow this ridge 10 miles to its eastern end, descend into the California Creek drainage, and hike out to Girdwood. This makes for an all-day outing; plan your route carefully. Most people will prefer to turn back at Penguin or after exploring the ridge a few miles past the peak.

44 | BIRD PEAK

Distance: 15 miles
Elevation Gain: 5700 feet
Hiking Time: 12 to 16 hours (or overnight)
Hike Difficulty: difficult
Terrain: rough trail, backcountry, scree, scrambling
High Point: 5505 feet
USGS Maps: Anchorage A-7, Seward D-7

Bird Peak, imposing and remote, is the most arduous trip in this book. The highest point in a vast circular drainage, Bird reigns over some of the park's most rugged terrain. This route takes you through an overgrown trail and across brushy hillsides to a secluded high valley, up jumbled scree slopes, and finally along a rocky summit ridge so precipitous on one side that it makes the entire peak seem cantilevered. Only strong hikers with some routefinding skills should attempt this trip. Although you can make it in very long day, you're better off camping for a night in the

Climbing Bird Peak's imposing summit pinnacle

beautiful high valley and tackling the summit pinnacle the next morning.

Getting There: Bird Creek Valley Trailhead. Drive south on the Seward Highway out of Anchorage. Continue past Bird Creek and nearby Bird Creek Recreation Site. One-half mile further, turn left on Konikson Road, just past a gas station. Follow this nondescript dirt road for ½ mile to where it dead-ends in a large gravel parking area. Chugach State Park signs mark the trailhead.

Follow the main dirt road north from the parking lot. Take an immediate right fork. Stay on this path, ignoring smaller cutoffs. After 1½ miles, cross Penguin Creek on a wide metal bridge. Turn right at the next fork and follow the slowly bending road into Penguin Creek Valley.

The trail, until now an easily traveled dirt road, gradually degenerates into a small, brush-choked path. A canopy of trees lowers across the trail, hanging right at eye level. Devil's club lines the trail's edges. Expect these worsening conditions to continue for 2½ miles. The trail splits at one point, but the forks rejoin shortly. Not far from this point, the trail suddenly ends. Look carefully and you'll find a game trail that takes a sharp left turn uphill. After about ⅛ mile on this path, you'll gratefully emerge above tree line into views of Penguin Peak and Turnagain Arm.

From here the game trail heads east along the hillside through high grasses. The trail is small, but ample enough to make the walking easy and simplify the routefinding. Follow it across another ½ mile of grassy slopes until it disappears in the middle of a wide, clear avalanche chute. One final ridge now divides you from the high valley beneath Bird Peak. It's important to gain some elevation here, though, and enter that valley above brush line; otherwise you'll earn yourself a nightmarish Alaskan bushwhacking story to share with the sourdoughs upon your return. Climb about 1000 feet up the avalanche chute, angling eastward toward a large knob protruding from the ridge. The hillside flattens noticeably above this knob. Continue traversing east on these gentler, bare slopes, and soon you'll drop into the high valley.

If you've scouted your route properly, you'll enter the valley at a broad flat area above almost all of the brush. With readily available water and total seclusion, this spot makes an ideal campsite. Relax during the long hours of summer twilight beneath the awe-inspiring western ridge of Bird Peak.

From here, an entirely different kind of trek begins, up loose rock and a long ridge to the summit. Start by gaining Bird's southwestern ridge near the prominent Point 4840. There are several ways to do so. For the easiest route, follow the stream upvalley as it disappears underneath a boulder field. Continue past a wide scree slope and around a bend. Beyond this bend, climb the buttressing ridge that rises to Point 4840. The ridge is somewhat steep but provides good footing.

From Point 4840, dip northeast into a saddle, and then begin the dramatic final ascent to Bird Peak. The western side of this ridge turns frighteningly vertical, but to the east lies a mellow slope. Some easy scrambling brings you to the false summit; the true summit, marked with a cairn, is ¼ mile east across rocky terrain. Pick your way over several mounds to the highest pinnacle, marked by a large cairn, and congratulate yourself on persevering through this difficult climb.

One final note: on the way down, be sure to locate the avalanche chute you climbed during the ascent. Descend with vigilance as you return to the game trail leading back below tree line. It is difficult to find but the only way to sanely navigate the brush-choked lower valley.

45 | HISTORIC IDITAROD (CROW PASS) TRAIL

From Girdwood to Eagle River
Distance: 26 miles (one way)
Elevation Gain: 1900 feet
Hiking Time: 1 to 3 days
Hike Difficulty: moderate
Terrain: established trail
High Point: 3500 feet
USGS Map: Anchorage A-6

Crow Pass
Distance: 8 miles
Elevation Gain: 1900 feet
Hiking Time: 4 to 6 hours
Hike Difficulty: moderate
Terrain: established trail
High Point: 3500 feet
USGS Map: Anchorage A-6

For a grand tour of the best Chugach State Park has to offer, head to the Historic Iditarod Trail. More commonly known as the Crow Pass Trail, it leads through quiet stands of birch; over a swift, cold river; and past high valleys, deep gorges, sapphire-blue tarns, and an immense glacier. Add several jagged peaks and scattered remnants of Alaska's gold mining days, and you're in for an unbeatable backpacking experience. Regular maintenance and heavy traffic (by Alaskan standards, that is) make the Historic Iditarod Trail less remote and wild than other hikes in this guide, but do not even think about missing it. You'll be hard pressed to find a lover of Chugach State Park who hasn't hiked this trail multiple times.

The Iditarod Trail is rich in history. In 1896, prospectors struck gold in Crow Creek, which eventually became the most productive placer gold

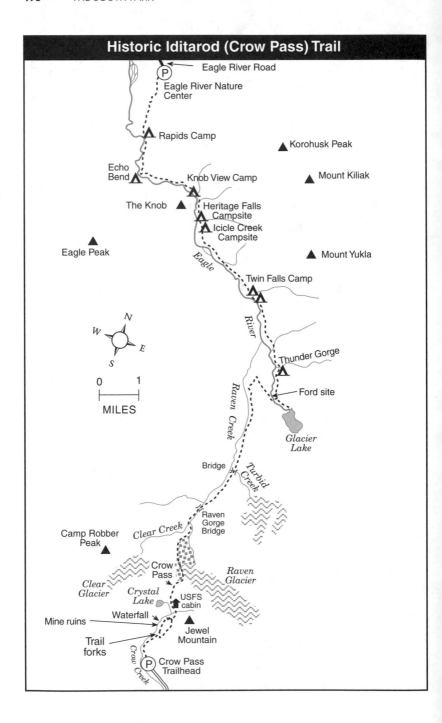

Historic Iditarod (Crow Pass) Trail

Eagle River Road
Eagle River Nature Center
Rapids Camp
Korohusk Peak
Echo Bend
Knob View Camp
Mount Kiliak
The Knob
Heritage Falls Campsite
Icicle Creek Campsite
Eagle Peak
Eagle
Mount Yukla
Twin Falls Camp
River
N
W   E
S
Thunder Gorge
0   1
MILES
Raven Creek
Ford site
Glacier Lake
Bridge
Turbid Creek
Camp Robber Peak
Clear Creek
Raven Gorge Bridge
Clear Glacier
Crow Pass
Raven Glacier
Crystal Lake
USFS cabin
Mine ruins
Waterfall
Jewel Mountain
Trail forks
Crow Creek
Crow Pass Trailhead

stream in Southcentral Alaska. Crow Creek's Monarch Mine was in full production even before the famous 1898 Klondike gold rush, and operated intermittently until 1940. Remnants of the mine, rusted relics of a lost era, still clutter the upper valley. Crow Pass's first recorded crossing was in 1898, when geologist Walter Mendenhall and his assistant Luther "Yellowstone" Kelly braved dense underbrush and voracious mosquitoes to find an overland route from Turnagain Arm to Knik. Once established, their route saw several years of heavy use, primarily from prospectors heading north to the gold fields of Nome and Iditarod. The trail eventually fell out of favor as later travelers opted for the longer but safer route over Indian Creek Pass. After years of neglect, the original Iditarod Trail all but disappeared until the Girl Scouts of America reestablished it in the 1970s. Now the trail and the pass have found new life as a hiker's paradise.

Most people complete the hike in 3 relaxed days, though 2-day and even single-day crossings are feasible. (In fact, elite runners competing in the annual Crow Pass Crossing finish it in as little as 3 hours!) If you plan to do the entire trail in 1 day, get an early start and travel light, but bring the Ten Essentials, a pair of sandals or sneakers for the river crossing, and twice as much food as you think you'll need. Most hikers walk north from Girdwood to Eagle River because the total elevation gain is less in this direction, and because the pay phone at the Eagle River Nature Center makes coordinating a trailhead pickup easier. Yet there is also something to be said for starting in Eagle River and hiking the trail in reverse. In this direction, the trail climbs steadily through successive biomes and reaches its physical and aesthetic high point (Crow Pass) near the end rather than at the beginning. The extra elevation becomes negligible when spread out over so many miles.

Of course, you need not hike the whole trail. Excellent out-and-back trips are possible at either end. From Girdwood, hike to Crow Pass in an easy afternoon, lounge at Crystal Lake, and perhaps climb a nearby mountain. Start at Eagle River for walks of a different character, where you can hike through serene forests at the river's edge and camp in the shadow of forbidding peaks named Korohusk, Kiliak, and Yukla—all derived from Dena'ina words meaning "evil spirits."

Getting There: Crow Pass Trailhead. Drive south from downtown Anchorage on the Seward Highway. At mile 90, turn left onto the Alyeska Highway. After 2 miles, turn left at a marked intersection onto Crow Creek Road. Continue on Crow Creek Road for 6 miles, ignoring a turnoff for the Crow Creek Mine. The main road ends at a gate; turn right onto a narrower road and continue 1 more mile to a large parking area at the trailhead.

Begin your trek at Crow Pass Trailhead and follow a series of switchbacks leading uphill. The trail soon climbs out of the brush, then rounds a corner into the upper Crow Creek Valley. After 1¼ mile, you'll reach a fork. Turn right to head directly to the pass, or continue straight for a slightly longer route that swings by the mine ruins, where a large boiler and metal

Bridge spanning Raven Gorge

pipes litter the area. Explore the hillside above the boiler and you'll find old tin cans, tools, and random junk. One person's trash is another person's historical artifact, so please don't take any "souvenirs" (or add to them, for that matter).

From the mine ruins, the trail climbs steeply through a series of switchbacks and into a high cirque, crosses Crow Creek above an impressive waterfall (the route up Jewel Mountain splits off here; see Hike 46), and then climbs to Crystal Lake. Just east of the lake you'll find a U.S. Forest Service cabin with one of the most spectacular front-porch views you could imagine. (To reserve it, call 1-800-280-2267. Unsurprisingly, the cabin is usually booked months in advance.) Crow Pass receives incredible amounts of snow, so don't be surprised to find the cabin still half buried in June, or to see the roof of the cabin's outhouse barely poking out of the snow at your feet. The heavy snowfall also leads to serious avalanche danger—best to take your winter outings elsewhere.

The trail, often soggy at this point, heads north from the cabin across a high rocky plateau dotted with tarns before reaching the pass proper, 3½ miles from the trailhead. You'll know you have arrived when, weather permitting, Raven Glacier comes suddenly into view. Fog, high winds, and rain are common at the pass—dress appropriately.

Cairns mark the trail as it crosses over the pass and descends into Raven Creek Valley. Here it skirts several rocky (and sometimes snow-covered) slopes, which can be wet and slippery. About 1 mile after the pass, just before the trail descends more steeply, you can continue traversing across the hillside to visit Clear Creek Valley (Hike 47). The main trail descends to Raven Creek, where you'll find a good spot for pitching a tent. Cross Clear Creek just before its confluence with Raven Creek and pick up the trail on the opposite bank. At mile 6.5 you'll reach Raven Gorge Bridge, spanning the swirling, violent waters of precipitous Raven Gorge. Across the gorge, the trail begins a long and steady descent through tall grasses and fireweed. Moose and bears are abundant, so be sure to announce your presence. At mile 8 a second bridge crosses Turbid Creek, which drains a massive glacier hanging several thousand feet above. This is the last spot for water before the Eagle River ford site.

The next 3 miles descend slowly through higher brush and scattered trees. There are several potential camping spots along this segment, but the area nearer to Eagle River offers better sites. At mile 11.5, the trail turns sharply and rapidly descends into the broad Eagle River Valley. Near the river, the trail disappears in tall brush. Follow periodic florescent tape and other markers east to reach the river. Large poles on each bank mark the ford site. Fording Eagle River can be dangerous if the water is running high (usually later in the day and earlier in the summer), and at no time should the crossing be taken lightly. Cross straight from pole to pole and exercise extreme caution (see the "Before You Go" section of the introduction for a review of river crossings).

Across the river, the trail enters scattered birch and alder. Shortly beyond the ford site, a small trail leads ½ mile east to Glacier Lake. The lake makes a pleasant side trip, and has ground suitable for camping. The main trail parallels Eagle River for the next 10 miles, punctuated here by several tributary stream crossings, some of which can be tricky in high water. Several sections of the trail follow uncomfortably near Eagle River's eroding bank, but mostly it's a gentle and pleasant walk. At mile 13.8 is Thunder Gorge, the first of several established campsites, complete with fire pits and cleared areas for tents. Several more campgrounds lie further down the trail: Twin Falls Camp at mile 16.4 (beneath mighty Mount Yukla), Icicle Creek Camp at mile 19.3, Heritage Falls Camp at mile 19.7, and Knob View Camp at mile 20.5. Dense vegetation along this stretch of the trail makes camping outside of an established campsite difficult, and doing so dramatically increases the impact on an already heavily used area. Please stick to the established sites or camp on a gravel bar along the river.

Around mile 20, just past a point called The Knob, the valley abruptly changes character, widening into a broad alluvial plain. The trail diverges from the river into mixed stands of spruce, quaking aspen, birch, and hemlock. At mile 22 it reaches the campsite at Echo Bend, a common turn-

around point for day hikers starting from Eagle River. A short distance farther is Rapids Camp, the last of the established campsites, at mile 23.3.

The final 2 miles climb slowly along a wide trail through boggy woods
to the Eagle River Nature Center, where civilization (including a pay
phone) awaits. If you're waiting for a ride, consider exploring more of the
Eagle River Trails (Hike 12). Otherwise, have a cup of coffee and peruse
the Nature Center's exhibits, or check out the telescope on the viewing deck
and look back upon your route through the park's Grand Tour.

46 | JEWEL MOUNTAIN

Distance: 6 miles
Elevation Gain: 3200 feet
Hiking Time: 5 to 7 hours
Hike Difficulty: moderate to difficult
Terrain: alpine tundra, scree, scrambling
High Point: 4800 feet
USGS Map: Anchorage A-6

Although Crow Pass often throngs with hikers, nearby Jewel Mountain remains overlooked and rarely visited. It was not always such a quiet place,
however. The mountain's western slopes—dotted with old trails, littered
with rusted cans, punctured by mine shafts—attest to a different era, when
miners spent decades digging through Jewel's heaps of scree in search of
gold. Although Jewel's mining days are long past, it now offers something
even more valuable: solitude.

This isn't a trip for the beginner. Climbing Jewel requires some scrambling, and takes you closer to a glacier's edge than some might care to
go. The upper part of the route can stay snowy late into the summer. But
navigate carefully and you'll find Jewel's secluded summit just a short
walk from the well-worn Iditarod Trail.

Getting There: Crow Pass Trailhead. Drive south from downtown
Anchorage on the Seward Highway. At mile 90, turn left onto the Alyeska
Highway. After 2 miles, turn left at a marked intersection onto Crow
Creek Road. Continue on Crow Creek Road for 6 miles, ignoring a turnoff for Crow Creek Mine. The main road ends at a gate; turn right onto a
narrower road and continue 1 more mile to a large parking area at the
trailhead.

From the trailhead, follow the Historic Iditarod Trail (also known as the
Crow Pass Trail) through wooded switchbacks into the open, upper valley.
Proceed past mine ruins to a second set of switchbacks that climb beside a
brilliant waterfall. Above the switchbacks, just before the trail crosses Crow

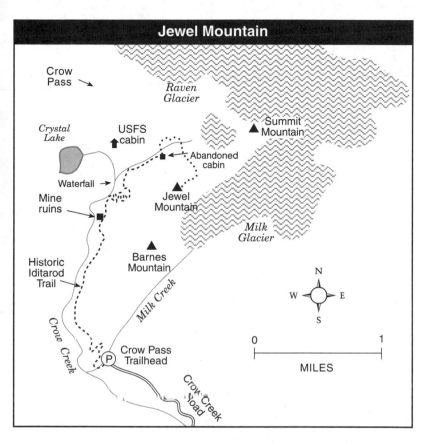

Jewel Mountain

Crow Pass

Raven Glacier

Crystal Lake

USFS cabin

Summit Mountain

Abandoned cabin

Waterfall

Mine ruins

Jewel Mountain

Milk Glacier

Historic Iditarod Trail

Barnes Mountain

Milk Creek

N
W E
S

Crow Creek

Crow Pass Trailhead

P

Crow Creek Road

0   1
MILES

Creek, turn right and, leaving the trail behind, hike straight uphill on rocky slopes. Very shortly you'll intersect a trail running parallel to the main trail you just left. Turn left (north) on this higher trail and follow it several hundred yards to a small cirque.

From the cirque, look at the steep slope on your right. Several streams cascade down the rocky slope; scramble up the rocks immediately to the right of the nearest stream. Be especially careful here, as the rock is often wet. After a short scramble up these rocks you'll reach a third trail, running parallel to the ones below. Turn left again and follow it north for another several hundred yards into a second, higher cirque. Here, perched near the top of the rocky slope you just climbed, is a splendidly dilapidated cabin. Its environs are strewn with rusting debris from the miners' lives.

The north face of Jewel Mountain rises behind the cabin in a crumbling mass of avalanche-prone slopes and rocky outcroppings. Thankfully, this is not your route; gentler slopes lead around to Jewel's eastern side, where you'll find a broad ridge running to the summit. Head northeast

Climbing scree on Jewel Mountain

from the cabin (crossing to the north side of the nearby stream) and climb to the ridge directly across the cirque. This ridge runs from a short peak directly north of Jewel Mountain to a low point between Jewel and Summit Mountains. Follow the ridge southward as it skirts the edge of a small glacier (keep off the ice!). You'll soon reach the stream you crossed earlier, near the cabin. Climb a short, steep section next to the stream to a flatter area above. Here, cross back over the stream and continue south up a final slope to the base of Jewel Mountain's east ridge. Snow often persists on this slope year-round.

You should now be at a broad saddle between Jewel Mountain and a high point on the ridge to distant Summit Mountain. The route described above, from the miners' cabin to this saddle, is not very distinct; let the conditions and your common sense dictate exactly how to go. If significant amounts of snow remain in the higher cirque, especially in early spring, there may be an avalanche risk.

Once at the saddle, turn right and climb the ridge to the southwest. It's a bit steep and drops off sharply to the south, but solid footing is easy to find. The final climb to Jewel's summit snakes through a maze of jumbled, fractured boulders, where some scrambling might be necessary.

The summit of Jewel Mountain reveals a contrast typical of Chugach State Park: to the west is Crow Pass and the mine ruins, cluttered with signs of humanity past and present. To the east, 1000 dizzying feet below, lies massive Milk Glacier, burying an entire valley in tons upon tons of ice. Ringed by jagged peaks and reaching finger-like from a land of eternal snow, this glacier is not visible from the Historic Iditarod Trail—or just about anywhere else frequented by people.

47 | CAMP ROBBER PEAK AND ARCHANGEL LAKES

Camp Robber Peak
Distance: 14 miles
Elevation Gain: 4700 feet
Hiking Time: 8 to 12 hours
Hike Difficulty: moderate to difficult
Terrain: rough trail, scree
High Point: 5855 feet
USGS Map: Anchorage A-6

Archangel Lakes
Distance: 16 miles
Elevation Gain: 4100 feet
Hiking Time: 10 to 13 hours (or overnight)
Hike Difficulty: moderate to difficult
Terrain: rough trail, scree
High Point: 5200 feet
USGS Map: Anchorage A-6

High in Clear Creek Valley, a remote glacier sits atop bare cliffs, spilling ice and water down hundreds of feet. Few animals and even fewer humans ever see it, as most eschew this rugged valley in favor of more gentle

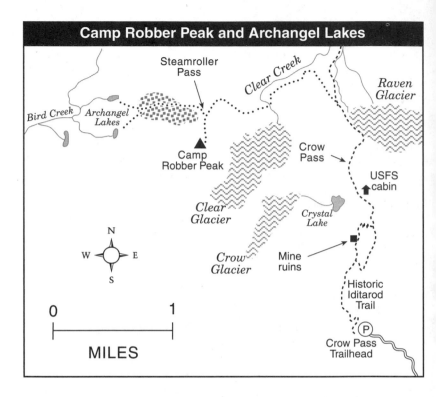

Camp Robber Peak and Archangel Lakes

Steamroller Pass
Clear Creek
Raven Glacier
Bird Creek
Archangel Lakes
Camp Robber Peak
Crow Pass
USFS cabin
Clear Glacier
Crystal Lake
N
W E
S
Crow Glacier
Mine ruins
Historic Iditarod Trail
0 1
MILES
P
Crow Pass Trailhead

terrain. Like many of the park's hidden corners, Clear Creek Valley remains largely untouched. But you can easily explore this valley on a day hike from Girdwood, or as side trip from the Historic Iditarod Trail. Make a short trip to the glacier, or press on to Steamroller Pass, a high saddle dividing the Raven Creek and Bird Creek watersheds. From there, follow a ridge to Camp Robber Peak, or descend to the diminutive Archangel Lakes. In either case, expect rugged terrain and solitude.

Getting There: Crow Pass Trailhead. Drive south from downtown Anchorage on the Seward Highway. At mile 90, turn left onto the Alyeska Highway. After 2 miles, turn left at a marked intersection onto Crow Creek Road. Continue on Crow Creek Road for 6 miles, ignoring a turnoff for Crow Creek Mine. The main road ends at a gate; turn right onto a narrower road and continue 1 more mile to a large parking area at the trailhead.

Hike along the Historic Iditarod Trail for 3½ miles to Crow Pass. Continue over the pass and follow the trail as it traverses a hillside above Raven Creek. About 1 mile after the pass, and shortly beyond a large cairn, the trail bends right and descends to the valley floor. At this bend, leave the trail and continue traversing across the hillside toward Clear Creek Valley. The valley is obvious (it's the first major valley on the left after the

pass), and the traversal is short and easy. If you prefer not to traverse sloping ground, or if you're approaching from the north on the Historic
Iditarod Trail, follow Clear Creek (the first tributary stream south of Raven
Gorge Bridge) up the valley from its confluence with Raven Creek. Expect
a small amount of bushwhacking.

However you get to Clear Creek Valley, you'll be struck by its isolation:
though so near to busy Crow Pass, it remains a hidden sanctuary above the
trees. Below the steep, truncated horizon there is little movement, and even
less sound.

For the easiest walking on the valley floor, stay above and to the left of
Clear Creek on a brushy plateau. Slightly upvalley, the creek curls left beneath steep mountain walls. Beyond this bend, ice-blue Clear Glacier
perches atop a rock face ¼ mile wide. A dozen tiny streams cascade from
the glacier down this rock face like haphazard fountains. You can climb up
to the foot of the glacier by skirting the right side of the face, but do not
walk on the glacier itself.

Continue to Steamroller Pass by climbing a gully in the western valley
wall just before the glacier. You'll need to ford Clear Creek; do so shortly
before the rock face, just past the point where the creek splits into two channels. The left channel forks several more times within about fifty feet. Cross

View from Clear Creek Valley

these smaller channels and then the main right fork. Immediately after crossing, turn right and head toward the obvious gully.

The gully bends first right, then sharply left toward the pass. It's a 1200-foot climb to the pass, but it is not overly steep and the footing is generally good. At the pass, a makeshift stone wall shields a potential campsite from the constant wind. Camp Robber Peak rises just south of the pass, and a collection of tiny tarns, the Archangel Lakes, lies westward.

To reach Camp Robber Peak, follow a flat bench on the western side of the main ridge from Steamroller Pass. It leads south to a small, high saddle between Camp Robber Peak and a false summit to the east. Turn right at this saddle and climb the final 300 feet to the peak.

Aside from a lack of water, Steamroller Pass makes an excellent campsite—but the Archangel Lakes are even better. To reach them, descend west from the pass. The first section is steep, so use caution. Once on flat ground, cross a mound of boulders (the leavings of a melted glacier) and continue down to the lakes. Remote and pristine, they are a wonderful place to camp. Most hikers will want to spend the night and then return as they came, over Steamroller Pass. But these quiet lakes can also mark the beginning of a long backcountry adventure. Try following Bird Creek from its source to its mouth, or climbing over Bird Pass into the Ship Creek headwaters. Wherever you go, don't expect much of a trail, and come prepared.

48 | GRIZZLY BEAR LAKE

Distance: 19 miles
Elevation Gain: 3900 feet
Hiking Time: 12 to 15 hours (or overnight)
Hike Difficulty: difficult
Terrain: rough trail, scree, backcountry
High Point: 4800 feet
USGS Map: Anchorage A-6

Plan well before undertaking a hike to Grizzly Bear Lake. To reach the lake, you'll have to cross miles of untracked backcountry, climb over a steep pass, and pick your way through a daunting moraine field. And that's the easy route! Because it is so difficult to reach, Grizzly Bear Lake is among the wildest spots in Chugach State Park. The small signs of human presence one expects to find in the more traveled parts of the park—a rusted tin can from a decade-old hunter's camp, an overturned rock once used to pin down a flapping tent—are entirely absent. Wilderness sprawls around the lake on all sides, devoid of human imprint.

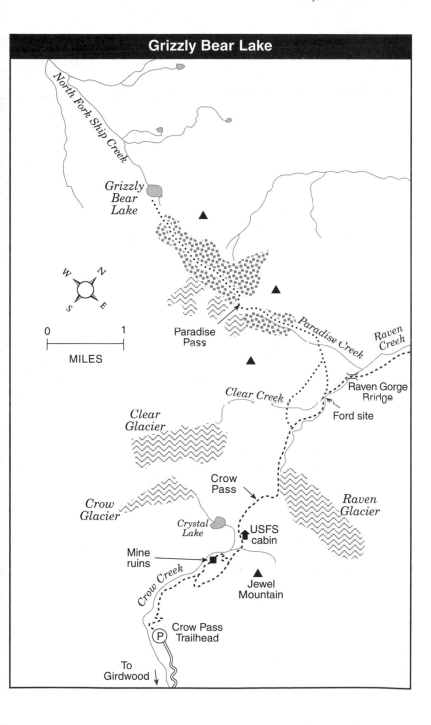

Grizzly Bear Lake

North Fork Ship Creek

Grizzly
Bear
Lake

N W E S

0   1
MILES

Paradise
Pass

Paradise Creek

Raven
Creek

Raven Gorge
Bridge

Clear Creek

Ford site

Clear
Glacier

Crow
Pass

Crow
Glacier

Raven
Glacier

Crystal
Lake

USFS
cabin

Mine
ruins

Crow Creek

Jewel
Mountain

Crow Pass
Trailhead

P

To
Girdwood

Getting There: Crow Pass Trailhead. Drive south from downtown Anchorage on the Seward Highway. At mile 90, turn left onto the Alyeska Highway. After 2 miles, turn left at a marked intersection onto Crow Creek Road. Continue on Crow Creek Road for 6 miles, ignoring a turnoff for Crow Creek Mine. The main road ends at a gate; turn right onto a narrower road and continue 1 more mile to a large parking area at the trailhead.

The first 3½ miles of this hike follow the Historic Iditarod Trail to Crow Pass. Continue over the pass as the trail descends past Raven Glacier and traverses the hillside above Raven Creek. About 1 mile after the pass, and shortly beyond a giant cairn, the trail bends right and descends toward the valley floor. At this point, leave the trail and, keeping a constant elevation, head left across the hillside toward Clear Creek Valley. The valley is obvious and the traversal is short and easy. After ¼ mile you'll be standing on the banks of Clear Creek.

Your next task is to reach Paradise Creek, found in the hanging valley 1 mile to the north. Cross Clear Creek, leaving Clear Creek Valley behind, and continue traversing northward above Raven Creek Valley at a constant elevation of about 3200 feet. (This traversal should not be attempted if the hillside is still covered in snow.) Paradise Creek Valley should also be obvious and, once you have it in sight, aim for the lip of this hanging valley.

(An alternate route to Paradise Creek avoids this sloping traverse but requires an additional 800 feet of elevation gain. Continue following the Iditarod Trail to the Raven Creek ford site at the confluence of Raven and Clear Creeks. After fording the creek, strike up the hillside to your left, angling diagonally toward Paradise Creek Valley. This may involve some light bushwhacking.)

The lower Paradise Creek Valley is aptly named. The mouth of this wide, grassy valley makes an ideal campsite with level ground, a peaceful stream, and a tremendous view across Raven Creek Valley. The valley mouth is about 6½ miles from the trailhead; a mid-afternoon start to your hike should put you at Paradise Creek Valley just in time to pitch camp.

To reach Grizzly Bear Lake, follow Paradise Creek up the valley. It's a smooth walk—at first. After a mile the reverie is broken by a rugged moraine field. The air grows colder, the tundra gives way to scree, and the colors change from verdant green to dull-gray rock. Continue over this broken terrain to a cirque at the head of the valley, where you'll see a once-massive glacier slowly melting its way out of existence.

The cirque walls rise steeply on all sides, but less so to the west. Paradise Pass is the low point along the western wall, although it's not much lower than the rest of the jumbled ridge and is difficult to pick out. Once you've identified the pass, look for a moraine bench running along the right wall of the cirque. Rather than cutting directly across the cirque basin, take the slightly longer route along this bench to its terminus just below the pass. This leaves you with only about 100 feet of steep and rocky terrain to

Quiet wilderness surrounds Grizzly Bear Lake.

ascend. Climb carefully, especially if you're toting a full pack.

A small glacier lies on the far side of the pass, just to the south. USGS topographical maps indicate that this glacier fully blocks the pass and extends for about ½ mile further north. Luckily, the glacier has retreated rapidly, and Paradise Pass is now open for business. Views from the pass are spectacular, and careful observers will count at least nine glaciers from this high vantage point, including massive Whiteout Glacier to the east.

From the pass, carefully descend westward. This side is slightly steeper and may have snow in early summer. However, it's only a short descent to the moraine below. Once on level ground, check your bearings and cut westward across the moraine to Grizzly Bear Lake, about 2 miles distant. Remote and pristine, Grizzly Bear Lake sits atop a high bend at the end of the valley. As you make camp, keep in mind that the terrain around the lake is extremely fragile.

Most hikers will want to return the easiest way and retrace their steps to Crow Pass Trailhead. But if you're up for a demanding backcountry expedition, continue westward into the grand North Fork Ship Creek Valley.

Expect some bushwhacking, although the walking is decent on a high bench along the valley's south side. You could roam for days through this sprawling wilderness; possible destinations include the Ewe Valley backcountry (Hike 19) and Indian Creek Pass. Wherever you go, you're not likely to forget the wild beauty of this valley.

49 | MOUNT ALYESKA

Ski Chalet
Distance: 1½ to 2 miles (one way)
Elevation Gain: 2000 feet
Hiking Time: 1 to 2 hours
Hike Difficulty: moderate
Terrain: established trail
High Point: 2200 feet
USGS Map: Seward D-6

Mount Alyeska
Distance: 3 miles (one way; 1 mile from chalet)
Elevation Gain: 3600 feet
Hiking Time: 4 to 6 hours
Hike Difficulty: moderate to difficult
Terrain: alpine tundra, scrambling
High Point: 3939 feet
USGS Map: Seward D-6

Visit Mount Alyeska and you'll find a touch of the Swiss Alps: a chalet, complete with a four-star restaurant, sits halfway up the mountain. You can either reach it the old-fashioned way (on foot), or hitch a lift on the Alyeska Tram and enjoy a graceful ride high above the ski slopes. From the chalet, take a short walk to a small glacier or spend an afternoon climbing Alyeska's southwestern ridge. Whether you walk or ride up the mountain, the tram (which is free on the way down) makes for a scenic and speedy descent. The hike starts at the Alyeska Prince Hotel.

Getting There: The Alyeska Prince Hotel. Follow the Seward Highway southbound from Anchorage for 37 miles. At milepost 90, turn left onto the Alyeska Highway toward Girdwood. Continue on this road 3 miles to Alyeska Resort and Ski Area. At a T intersection, turn left onto Arlberg Road. Follow this road to its end at the hotel and park in the hotel parking lot's visitor section.

If you'd like to ride the tram to the Seven Glaciers Restaurant, purchase a ticket at the hotel. (And if you're planning to descend via the tram, be sure to

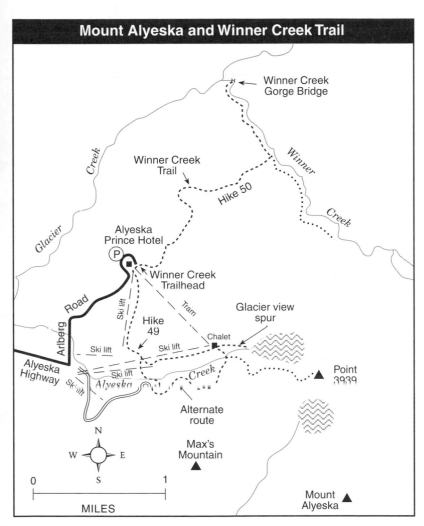

Mount Alyeska and Winner Creek Trail

Winner Creek Gorge Bridge

Winner Creek Trail

Hike 50

Winner Creek

Glacier Creek

Alyeska Prince Hotel

Winner Creek Trailhead

Glacier view spur

Tram

Arlberg Road

Ski lift

Hike 49

Chalet

Ski lift

Ski lift

Glacier view spur

Point 3939

Alyeska Highway

Ski lift

Ski lift

Alyeska Creek

Alternate route

N

W — E

S

Max's Mountain

0   1

MILES

Mount Alyeska

check the posted hours before departing, lest you find yourself unexpect-
edly descending on foot in darkness.) Otherwise, walk around the hotel to
the mountain side and start your hike on a gravel trail running beneath a
chair lift. Continue past the top of this chair lift and stay on the track as it
bends around the northern slopes of Alyeska. You'll soon pass under a second chair lift. From here, either turn left and follow small trails directly up
the ridge, or continue traversing until you cross Alyeska Creek and meet a
service road leading to the chalet. The service road adds about a mile onto
the trip, but it's gentler and easier to follow. The ridge route is direct but not
marked; use the second chair lift as a guide to the chalet.

The elegant Seven Glaciers Restaurant is situated on a 2200-foot high plateau with views of silt-gray Turnagain Arm and the high Chugach Mountains. You can relax at the restaurant bar with refreshments and snacks or on the tundra with a picnic lunch. Don't be surprised if you see someone suddenly fling herself off the hillside—this is a favorite launching site for paragliders. Kick back and watch them trace graceful arcs in the sky as they drift toward Girdwood. Before you leave, try to identify all seven glaciers supposedly visible from the restaurant. No one seems to know which to count—good luck!

Beyond the chalet lie several higher destinations. The first is a small glacier, ¼ mile away. Reach it via the upper gravel trail departing from the restaurant, which beelines to the glacier quickly and smoothly. Nestled in a steep-walled cirque, the glacier is a tiny reminder of the ice fields that once buried all of Southcentral Alaska. While this remnant is not the most impressive glacier in the area, the tram certainly makes it the easiest to reach. It's a great place to bring unathletic out-of-town guests.

A longer outing climbs a ridge to the false summit of Mount Alyeska. From the restaurant, follow the lower gravel trail (the service road) for a few hundred feet. Just after crossing Alyeska Creek, head off-trail and climb the ridge on your left, which rises 1500 feet to meet Alyeska's main southwestern ridge. At the ridge crest, turn left and continue to Point 3939. Expect about 10 feet of easy scrambling. Stop at this false summit— the ridge to Alyeska's true peak is usually corniced and should not be attempted without the proper equipment and experience. However, even

Ski chalet high on Mount Alyeska

from Point 3939 you'll have views of the upper Winner Creek Valley and the distant Twentymile Creek wilderness. Return to the chalet the way you came.

50 | WINNER CREEK TRAIL

Distance: 5 miles round trip
Elevation Gain: 400 feet
Hiking Time: 2 to 3 hours
Hike Difficulty: easy
Terrain: established trail
High Point: 600 feet
USGS Map: Seward D-6

If you'd like a break from the hill climbs and high tundra typical of Chugach State Park, head to the Winner Creek Trail. Here, in the perpetual twilight of the boreal rain forest, a gentle trail winds through hulking, moss-coated spruce trees on the way to Winner Creek Gorge—a dramatic, churning cauldron of glacial meltwater. Though at times muddy and slippery, the trail is suitable for hikers of all abilities.

Getting There: The Alyeska Prince Hotel. Take the Seward Highway southbound out of Anchorage. At mile 90 (37 miles from Anchorage), turn left onto the Alyeska Highway and head into Girdwood. Follow this road 3 miles to Alyeska Resort and Ski Area, then turn left at the stop sign onto Arlberg Road. Follow Arlberg to its end at the hotel and park in the hotel parking lot's visitor section.

The Winner Creek Trail follows a section of the original Iditarod Trail that ran from Seward to Nome. Start your hike directly behind the Alyeska Prince Hotel, where a National Forest sign marks the trailhead (the hike actually lies within Chugach National Forest, not Chugach State Park). A short gravel trail leads into the woods. This well-maintained path meanders through the dense forest, crossing muddy stretches on boardwalks. Watch out for wet rocks and boards, which can be very slippery. Several smaller trails branch off from time to time, but the main trail makes no sharp turns and should be obvious.

After 1 mile the trail reaches a signposted intersection at Winner Creek. Make a mental note of the intersection so as not to miss it on your return. Bearing right at the intersection takes you several miles up a deteriorating trail, past an old cabin, and into a high alpine valley. Only hikers willing to bushwhack will want to venture far in this direction, where dramatic views of the rugged Twentymile Creek wilderness compensate for the more difficult travel.

Most hikers will want to head to Winner Creek Gorge. Bear left and continue on the trail for 1 mile. The dull roar of rushing water precedes the gorge itself. A footbridge allows you to peer over the gorge's smooth rock walls and feel the cold, glistening spray of freshly melted snow and ice. It's a worthy alternative to a mountaintop and every bit as dramatic.

Dense old-growth rainforest lines the Winner Creek Trail.

APPENDIX A: FAVORITE HALF DAY, FULL DAY, AND OVERNIGHT TRIPS

OWEN'S FAVORITE HIKES

Half day:
Eklutna Lakeside Trail (Hike 2)
Even a brief walk along this crescent-shaped lake gives a sense of its beauty, tempered but never dampened by the seasonal changes. Majestic, icy-gray, and eerily opaque, Eklutna seems less a lake than an inland ocean.
Winner Creek Trail (Hike 50)
Though at times a little too trafficked, this short trail never fails to instill a sense of solitude, wandering among giant rain forest spruce and explosions of green moss. Winner Creek Gorge at trail's end is an intriguing sight.

Full day:
Pioneer Ridge and South Summit (Hike 1)
You have to climb a long way, but the view from Pioneer Ridge makes every step worth it. The trail is mostly gentle, the footing solid, and the picnic tables make welcome rest stops for weary travelers. But best of all is the view of Mount Marcus Baker, lingering on the horizon like a distant dream, startlingly white.
Bird Peak (Hike 44)
Though it's a *very* long day and a *very* challenging hike, nothing compares to Bird Peak for rugged adventure. Most hikers will prefer to make this a two-day trip, allowing a gentler pace and exquisitely isolated camping, but some will want to go light and go fast in a single day. The final ascent to the summit is a stunning climax.

Overnight Trips:
Grizzly Bear Lake (Hike 48)
Hands down the wildest, most pristine spot you'll reach in the park without some serious bushwhacking. The barren lakeshore appears utterly untouched by humans. Let's try to keep it that way! The approach to Paradise Pass is a wonderful hike in and of itself.
The Dome and Long Lake (Hike 23)
Far less visited than neighboring Williwaw Lakes Valley, North Fork Campbell Creek Valley is every bit as beautiful and only slightly harder to

reach. A great base camp for exploring and soaking up the wilderness right behind Anchorage.

SHANE'S FAVORITE HIKES

Half Day:
Eagle River Trails (Hike 12)
With the Eagle River Nature Center hosting so many different activities and maintaining a variety of lowland trails, this area of the park is a must-see. It's a great place for a relaxed evening hike or a short weekend outing coupled with one of the Nature Center's outdoor programs.
Bird Ridge (Hike 42)
Although reaching the ridge proper requires a steep elevation gain, the rewards come quickly—easy walking on the alpine tundra and magnificent views of Turnagain Arm. Watch the bore tides sweep up Turnagain Arm from the lower trail, or continue to Bird Ridge Overlook to watch the sun hanging low over the western Chugach Mountains.

Full Day:
Snow Hawk Valley and Temptation Peak (Hike 21)
With two isolated tarns, two cozy cabins, and one very large peak, you won't be short of places to visit in this wide valley. The cabins, seemingly dropped from the sky onto the sprawling tundra, provide comfort and a base for exploring the valley.
Bold Ridge Overlook (Hike 4)
Be sure to bring your camera on this one. Snap some photos of Bold Peak's massive northern face, then take in the full panorama of Eklutna Valley from atop the overlook. The lakeside approach, tree-shrouded ascent, and alpine tundra provide a variety typical of the park.

Overnight Trips:
Flute Glacier and Eagle Peak (Hike 17)
This is a trip through geologic time, following the path of a retreating glacier. Eagle Peak, one of the most challenging scrambles in the park, offers a superb lookout over Flute and Organ Glaciers.
Williwaw Lakes Trail and The Ballpark (Hike 33)
The Ballpark is possibly the strangest place in the western part of the park. Wander across the width of The Ballpark, taking in its unique knobs and ruts, and visit Deep Lake and Black Lake before descending to the placid Williwaw Lakes.

APPENDIX B: WHAT TO TAKE

Day Hike Equipment:

Day pack
Extra food
Sunglasses and sunscreen
First-aid kit
Pocketknife
Matches
Fire starter
Flashlight with extra batteries and bulb
Maps
Compass
Water and water purifier
Watch
Toilet paper
Proper footwear
Rain shell
Wool hat
Warm sweater or jacket

Additional Equipment for Overnight Trips:

Backpack with waterproof cover
Sleeping bag
Air mattress or foam pad
Tent and rainfly
Ground cloth
Full raingear
Gloves
Cooking and dishwashing utensils
Camp stove and fuel
Small towel

APPENDIX C: OUTDOOR OUTFITTERS AND COMMERCIAL CAMPGROUNDS IN ANCHORAGE

Alaska Mountaineering and Hiking
2633 Spenard Road
(907) 272-1811
www.alaskamountaineering.com

Recreational Equipment Inc.
1200 West Northern Lights Boulevard
(907) 272-4565

Centennial Park Campground
8300 Boundary Road
(907) 343-6986

Creekwood Inn
2150 Gambell
(907) 258-6006

Golden Nugget RV Park
4100 DeBarr Road
1-800-449-2012

John's RV Consignment
3453 Mountain View Drive
(907) 277-4332

APPENDIX D: ORGANIZATIONS CONCERNED WITH PROTECTING ALASKA'S WILDERNESS

Alaska Center for the Environment
519 West Eighth Avenue, #201
Anchorage, AK 99501
(907) 274-3621
   Anchorage-based group concerned with forest preservation, transportation planning, public lands, wildlife protection, and a number of other environmental issues facing Alaska.

Alaska Rain Forest Network
406 G Street
Anchorage, AK 99501
(907) 222-2552
www.akrain.org
   Coalition of conservation organizations working to protect Alaska's Tongass and Chugach National Forests.

Alaska Wilderness League
320 Fourth Street NE
Washington, DC 20002
(202) 544-5205
   Washington, D.C.-based group concerned primarily with the continued protection of the Arctic National Wildlife Refuge on Alaska's North Slope.

Alaska Wildlife Alliance
P.O. Box 202022
Anchorage, AK 99520-2022
(907) 277-0897
   Concerned with the conservation of Alaska's wildlife. Advocates an ecosystem approach to conservation representing the intrinsic value of wildlife in addition to its value to people.

Northern Alaska Environmental Center
218 Driveway Street
Fairbanks, AK 99701-2895
(907) 452-5021
www.northern.org
    Works to protect wilderness in Arctic and Interior Alaska.

The Sierra Club
85 Second Street, Second Floor
San Francisco, CA 94105-3441
(415) 977-5500
www.sierraclub.org
    National environmental organization dedicated to preserving wild lands, fighting sprawl, and improving air and water quality nationwide.

Greenpeace, USA (Alaska Office)
(907) 277-8234
    Branch of the international environmental group concerned with forests, marine habitat, energy, and toxic waste.

INDEX

ABOUT THE AUTHORS

Shane Shepherd and Owen Wozniak grew up hiking together throughout Chugach State Park. Owen recently completed a master's degree in environmental policy and now works to preserve wilderness and open urban space. He spends his free time (when not hiking!) watching movies and learning to surf. Shane graduated from Duke University with a degree in philosophy and is about to start a graduate program in finance. In his free time you might find him climbing at the local crags, at a nearby cafe writing away on his Powerbook, or, of course, wherever there are interesting trails to hike.

Owen Wozniak

Shane Shepherd

THE MOUNTAINEERS, founded in 1906, is a nonprofit outdoor activity and conservation club, whose mission is "to explore, study, preserve, and enjoy the natural beauty of the outdoors...." Based in Seattle, Washington, the club is now the third-largest such organization in the United States, with 14,000 members and seven branches throughout Washington State.

The Mountaineers sponsors both classes and year-round outdoor activities in the Pacific Northwest, which include hiking, mountain climbing, ski-touring, snowshoeing, bicycling, camping, kayaking and canoeing, nature study, sailing, and adventure travel. The club's conservation division supports environmental causes through educational activities, sponsoring legislation, and presenting i nformational programs. All club activities are led by skilled, experienced volunteers, who are dedicated to promoting safe and responsible enjoyment and preservation of the outdoors.

If you would like to participate in these organized outdoor activities or the club's programs, consider a membership in The Mountaineers. For information and an application, write or call The Mountaineers, Club Headquarters, 300 Third Avenue West, Seattle, Washington 98119; (206) 284-6310.

The Mountaineers Books, an active, nonprofit publishing program of the club, produces guidebooks, instructional texts, historical works, natural history guides, and works on environmental conservation. All books produced by The Mountaineers fulfill the club's mission.

Send or call for our catalog of more than 500 outdoor titles:

The Mountaineers Books
1001 SW Klickitat Way, Suite 201
Seattle, WA 98134
800-553-4453
mbooks@mountaineersbooks.org
www.mountaineersbooks.org